THE TEAM THAT WOULDN'T DIE

John Roberts was born in Stockport and joined the staff of his local paper, the *Stockport Express*, shortly after leaving school, becoming sports editor of the paper at the age of nineteen. At twenty-one he joined the sports desk of the *Daily Express* in Manchester. Since then he has written for the *Guardian* and the *Daily Mail* and is now the tennis correspondent of the *Independent*. He is married with three children.

JOHN ROBERTS

THE TEAM THAT WOULDN'T DIE

THE STORY OF THE BUSBY BABES

Introduction by Sir Matt Busby

VISTA

First published in Great Britain 1975
by Arthur Barker Ltd

This Vista edition published 1998
Vista is an imprint of the Cassell Group
Wellington House, 125 Strand, London WC2R 0BB

A catalogue record for this book is
available from the British Library.

ISBN 0 575 60270 8

Typeset by SetSystems, Saffron Walden
Printed and bound in Great Britain by
Cox & Wyman, Reading, Berks

98 99   10 9 8 7 6 5 4 3 2 1

TO PHYLLIS

My thanks go to Sir Matt Busby, Jimmy Murphy, Bill Foulkes, Manchester United, Captain Thain, Peter Ball, my friend Tony Jackson, the relatives and friends of the Munich victims and all who contributed to this book.

Contents

Illustrations

The author and publisher are grateful to the
Daily Express, Popperfoto and relatives of the Munich
victims for permission to reproduce the illustrations.

Author's note

This book was originally researched in 1974
and published in 1975, and apart from the
epilogue and final chapter remains unchanged.

Introduction

My memorial is the three great teams I created for Manchester United in twenty-three years of managership. But which of the three do I rate the best?

Old-timers may say the 1948 FA Cup-winning side, my first one. Younger ones and some old-timers will say the pre-Munich team, the Babes. And there are those who, because of the magic of Charlton, Law and Best, will say the European Cup-winning team of 1968, albeit without the injured Law.

They were all great teams, but I have no doubt in my mind at all. The pre-Munich team was potentially the best club side I have seen, about to take over that crown from Real Madrid when the Munich crash ended them.

I am delighted that John Roberts has written this book recalling that great team and those wonderful players.

It is a highly readable recollection of that period and some parts of the book were completely fresh and new to me, even though I was so deeply and personally involved.

SIR MATT BUSBY

1. Munich

The British European Airways twin-engine Elizabethan, RMA 'Lord Burleigh', G-ALZU AS 57, returning from a charter flight to Belgrade with Manchester United Football Club on board, had stopped to refuel at Munich airport. The time was 14.19 hours, 6 February 1958.

On the flight deck, Captain James Thain, who was in command and who had flown the aircraft to Belgrade, was sitting in the right-hand, first officer's seat. His friend, Captain Kenneth Rayment, who had taken the controls for the homeward journey, was sitting in the left-hand seat.

Captain Rayment requested permission to taxi the aircraft for take-off and was given clearance. Eleven minutes later the radio officer, William Rodgers, told the airport control tower that 609 Zulu Uniform was 'rolling'.

The events that followed are narrated by Captain Thain.

'As Ken opened the throttles, which were between us on the central pedestal, with his right hand, I followed with my left hand. When they were fully open I tapped his hand and held the throttles in the fully open position.

'Ken moved his hand and I called "Full power" and, looking at the instruments in front of me, said "Temperatures and pressures correct and warning lights out". I then called out the speed in knots as the aircraft accelerated.

'The engines sounded an uneven note and the needle on the port pressure gauge started to fluctuate. I felt a pain in my left hand as Ken pulled the throttles back and said "Abandon take-off". I held the control column fully forward while Ken put on the brakes.'

The aircraft was almost at a halt forty seconds after the start of its run.

'What had happened was boost surging, which was not uncommon with Elizabethans at the time, particularly at airports like Munich, because of their height above sea level.

'Over-rich mixture caused the power surge, but though the engines sounded uneven there was not much danger that the take-off power of the aircraft would be affected. The Elizabethans were very powerful in their day and you could actually have taken off on one engine.

'Knowing that one cause of boost surging was opening the throttles too quickly, Ken said that at the start of our next run he would open the throttles a little before releasing the brakes and then continue to open them more slowly.' Clearance for take-off was given a second time at 14.34 hours.

'Ken opened the throttles to twenty-eight inches, released the brakes, and off we went again.'

The aircraft came to a stop again forty seconds later.

'I took the decision to abandon the take-off this time. We were half-way down the runway with the throttles fully open when I saw the starboard engine steady itself at fifty-seven-and-a-half inches but the port pressure run to sixty inches and beyond. I wanted to discuss this with the BEA station engineer.'

The aircraft returned to the tarmac and Captain Thain took over the controls when they were clear of the runway, while Captain Rayment told the passengers over the address system that there was a technical fault. Captain Thain found it difficult to see the edge of the runway track because of snow.

Captain Rayment took the controls again and brought the aircraft to the airport buildings. Twenty minutes had elapsed since it had first left the buildings.

'The station engineer, William Black, came to the cockpit to check the trouble and we explained about the boost surging. He said it was fairly common at airports like Munich, above sea level, and described the recommended procedures to overcome it. We told him we had tried these without eliminating the noise.

'He said that re-tuning the engines would mean an overnight stop. I said I didn't think this was necessary because the starboard engine had performed normally.

'We talked about opening the throttles even more slowly and, after discussing the state of the runway, I said we would have another go at take-off. That's when we found we had no passengers. They had gone back to the airport lounge. The station engineer went to instruct the traffic officer to recall the passengers.

'Ken and I had not been out of the cockpit but talked about the snow and looked at the wings from the flight deck. We had lost the film of snow we had noticed before our first departure and decided there was no need to have the wings swept.'

At 14.56.30, Captain Rayment again requested permission to taxi out to runway 24/25. It was given and, after routine checks in the cockpit, the aircraft was ready for take-off at forty seconds past 15.00 hours and was 'rolling' at 15.03.06.

According to the official record: 'The last message from 609 Zulu Uniform starts with a howling, whistling noise and ends with a loud background noise after the message was broken off.'

On the flight deck the co-pilots started the third run.

'I told Ken that if we got boost surging again I would control the throttles. Ken opened them to twenty-eight inches with the brakes on, and both engine readings were steady. Ken released the brakes and we moved forward.

'Ken continued to open the throttles and again I followed with my left hand until the levers were fully open. I tapped his hand and he moved it. He called "Full power" and I checked the dials and said "Full power".

'The boost surging started again at eighty-five knots and I called out to Ken about it and pulled the port throttle lever back until the surging was controlled and the reading was fifty-four inches and then pushed the throttle back until it was fully open, fifty-seven-and-a-half inches throughout.'

Captain Thain called 'Full power' again and looked at the temperatures and pressures.

'I then glanced at the air speed indicator and saw it registered 105 knots and was flickering. When it reached 117 knots I called out "V1" (Velocity 1, which is the point on the runway after which it is unsafe to abandon take-off) and waited for a positive indication of more speed so that I could call "V2" (the speed required before taking off and in this case 119 knots).

'But suddenly the needle dropped to about 112 and then 105 knots. I had not looked out of the cockpit, but I had not felt anything that would have given the impression that we were losing acceleration.

'Once before I had experienced a failure of the air speed indicator at a similar stage of take-off. I had continued and the aircraft took off quite normally. On checking later, it had been found that an engineer working on the instruments had taken off the panel. But when he had replaced it he had somehow trapped a tube leading to the air speed indicator which had prevented the instrument from reading correctly.

'This flashed through my mind when I saw the indicator showing a loss of speed at Munich, though it could only have been the flash of a thought, because suddenly Ken shouted "Christ! We can't make it!"

'Until then I had been looking at the instruments. When Ken shouted I looked up and could see a lot of snow and a house and a tree right in the path of the aircraft.

'I took my left hand from behind the throttle levers and banged them, but they were fully forward. I think Ken was pulling the control column back. He asked for the under-carriage to be lifted and I selected "up".

'Then I put my hands out in front of me and gripped the ledge and peered over the edge. It seemed that we were turning to starboard and I was convinced we could not get between the house and the tree. I put my head down and waited for the impact of the crash.

'The aircraft went through a fence and crossed a road and the port wing hit the house. The wing and part of the tail were torn off and the house caught fire.'

In the house, mother-of-four Mrs Anna Winkler was sewing. Her husband was away and her eldest daughter was at a neighbour's house. She threw two of her sleeping children into the snow, and another four-year-old crawled out through a window.

'As the aircraft spun, a tree just further on than the house came through the port side of the flight deck where Ken was sitting. The starboard side of the fuselage hit a wooden hut, where there was a truck filled with tyres and fuel. This exploded.

'We were spinning and then the aircraft stopped. There was a hellish noise. And then complete silence.

'I shouted "Abandon aircraft". William Rodgers put off his switches and went out through the emergency window of the galley door. Ken couldn't leave his seat and was shouting that his foot was jammed. I went out through the emergency exit to inspect the fires. I expected the plane to go up unless the fires were put out and returned to the flight deck to collect the portable fire extinguisher and told Ken to hang on until the fires had been put out.

'I tried to get people out of the aircraft. I could see the bodies and tried to do what I could. It was chaos. Even when help arrived, people just seemed to stand open-mouthed in horror at it all. Some seemed in a daze. I got very irritated and very angry with some, but I suppose their reaction was understandable, suddenly arriving at a scene like that.

'At times I just couldn't get through to people to make them move to where they were needed. I remember snatching an axe off one man, running to where Ken was trapped and hacking away to get him out. The man seemed to get the message then.

'Ken's leg was broken in about five places and the tree had hit his head. When I went to the hospital I was told he would be OK. He was badly injured but they felt he would survive.

'He battled for three weeks before he finally died of brain damage.'

The Manchester United defender Bill Foulkes tells what it was like from his seat in the middle of the cabin.

'The flight from Belgrade was uneventful. I'd known worse. We played cards, as usual, and our mood was great. We were back in the European Cup semi-final and were thinking about beating Real Madrid to win it this time.

'Oh, yes, we had to beat Milano first, but we did not see that as any problem. Red Star were a better side than Milano, and we had handled them far easier than the 3–3 score in Belgrade suggested. And we were sure we would beat Madrid in the final.

'We had learned a lot and were twice as good as when we had met Madrid the previous year, losing 5–3 on aggregate. This was going to be our year.

'I had no worries about flying. They could turn the plane upside down and fly it that way for all I cared. If there was turbulence, or the plane hit an air pocket, it used to fascinate me. Those things never bothered me because I had complete faith in the aircraft.

'The journey was broken when the plane landed to refuel at Munich. We left the plane and had coffee. It was a very cold day. They had had to clear snow from the pitch in Belgrade before the match, and the weather had not improved.

'It was not long before we were called back to the plane, and it set off down the runway. The snow was coming down by this time. Despite a long run there was no take-off. The brakes went on, the plane came to a halt and turned back.

'This unsettled us, but the plane set off again. Not so far this time. And it stopped again. We were taken back to the airport building and ordered more coffee. After about fifteen minutes we were called back to the plane, but had to wait a few minutes for Alf Clarke of the *Manchester Evening Chronicle*.

'Alf had put a call through to his office. When he arrived, we prepared to take off again. There were no cards now. I had put them into their cardboard pack and slipped it into my right hip pocket. We were all apprehensive.

'I was sitting next to a window on the right-hand side of the gangway, half-way down the plane, with my back towards the cockpit. A wing was just above where I was sitting and I could see an engine. Ken Morgans was on my right and the other members of our card school, facing us, were David Pegg and Albert Scanlon.

'To our right was another school, on a six-seater. There were five of them, Roger Byrne, Billy Whelan, Dennis Viollet, Ray Wood and Jackie Blanchflower.

'Matt Busby and Bert Whalley were sitting behind us. Mark Jones, Tommy Taylor, Duncan Edwards and Eddie Colman were all at the back of the plane.

'David Pegg said "I'm not sitting here. It's not safe", and went to the back of the plane. And I seem to remember Frank Swift standing up near the back and saying something like "That's right, lads, this is the place to be".

'We set off and I remember looking out of the window. They had big windows, those Elizabethans. I remember seeing the snow coming down and the slush flying about and then there was a terrible noise, the kind you might expect to hear if a car suddenly left a smooth road and started running over rocks.

'Instinctively, I crouched down into my seat and fastened my seat belt really tight. There was a tremendous bang. I must have passed out for a minute or so, because the next thing I remember was looking ahead and seeing just a hole right in front of me. I had no grasp of what had happened. The back of the plane had just disappeared.

'I looked out of the window and saw smoke coming out of the engine. Then, Captain Thain, one of the pilots, was banging on the window shouting at me to get out.

'But when I tried to move, I couldn't. I started to panic and to feel for my legs in case something had happened to me. It was a while before I pulled myself together and realized the seat belt was keeping me down.

'I got out and just ran as fast as I could. I must have been thinking the plane might blow up at any second, but I can't remember having a clear thought in my head. I just ran and ran across a field and the snow became deeper and deeper.

'Then, I don't know why, I stopped and turned round. I could see the part of the plane I had left. Then, what seemed about a mile away, the back of the plane was ablaze in a petrol dump. All that could be seen of it clearly was the tail fin.

'People who saw the crash said later that the plane did not take off but sort of bounced off the runway, over a fence. It went on into a cottage, which was struck by part of a wing. This turned the plane and it started spinning towards the petrol dump, a trailer filled with fuel containers.

'On impact, the plane was torn apart, with the back exploding into the fuel dump and the front part spinning away.

'When I saw the tail blazing I started to move back. I then saw bodies. Roger Byrne, strapped in his seat, leaning over backwards as if his back was broken. Bobby Charlton, in another seat, not moving. And Dennis Viollet.

'Harry Gregg appeared suddenly, his face covered in blood. He looked in a bad way, but it turned out that he had only nicked a nostril. We found Jackie Blanchflower, with an arm bleeding badly. Harry tore a strip off something and tied a tourniquet round Jackie's arm. I kept telling Harry he was tying it too tight, but he didn't seem to hear. He didn't take any notice.

'I found Matt, lying on his side. He seemed semiconscious and I asked if he was all right. He just kept saying "My side . . . my side". I tried to put a coat under his side, because the ground was very wet, but he gave a terrible groan and I thought "What have I done?"

'Bobby Charlton appeared alongside me. I asked if he was all right. He just kept looking. Then a stretcher was put down. And another. And another.

'Someone told us to help lift Matt on to a stretcher, which we did. It was taken to a Volkswagen mini-bus with seats taken out of it. When the stretcher was in, Bobby Charlton and Dennis Viollet were told to sit in the front and I sat in a seat at the back.

'The mini-bus had not moved far when it was stopped, the back doors opened again and another stretcher, on which was Mrs Miklos, wife of the courier, badly burned, was placed alongside Matt.

'We started off again at high speed across the snow and slush. I thought the driver was going too fast for safety. I must have been in a state of shock, because after shouting at the driver to slow down and getting no response, I punched him on the back of the head. I must have thumped him half a dozen times, but he just ignored me. I shouted for Bobby and Dennis to do something. They just stared and looked vacant.

'When we reached hospital, the doors of the mini-bus were whipped open and the stretchers were carried away. I saw Harry Gregg, and we just seemed to wander down a hospital corridor, not really knowing what we were doing or where we were going.

'A nurse came out of a room and asked me to step inside. She pointed, asking "Who is that?" It was Johnny Berry. His head was tilted and his bottom teeth had cut through his upper mouth and into his nose. The nurse gave me a label and I wrote Johnny's name on it.

'I went back into the corridor and moved to catch up with the others. It was then, for the first time, that I noticed I had only one shoe. A wet sock was flapping on my other foot. I just pulled the sock up and joined the other lads.

'A nurse appeared, holding a big needle. She grabbed Bobby and gave him a jab. Harry and I weren't having any of that. We ran down the corridor and out of the hospital entrance and stood on the steps.

'After a while a BEA representative came along and asked us if we wanted to go into the hospital. We said we didn't, so she arranged for us to be taken to a hotel.

'I asked if she could get me some shoes, and she took the one I had left as a guide to the size, went to a store and brought me some fur-lined boots.

'When we were in the hotel room, Harry and I were in a daze. We didn't know what to do, and just followed each other around. I went to the toilet. Harry came with me. Then Harry went out on to the balcony, and I went with him.

'We shared a bottle of whisky, though I didn't usually drink in those days.

'Next day, we went back to the hospital. Matt was in an oxygen tent. Duncan Edwards was shouting "Let's have some bloody attention". The wards were small. I saw Bobby Charlton, with a bandaged head, and Jackie Blanchflower, nursing his arm. Dennis Viollet had a knock on his jaw and a gashed head. Albert Scanlon, who had been found under a wheel, had a fractured skull. Ray Wood had a gashed face and concussion. I remember also seeing Ken Morgans and Johnny Berry.

'I was talking to a nurse about Johnny and Duncan. She seemed to think Duncan's chances were better than Johnny's, but she was to be proved wrong.[1]

1. Duncan Edwards died on 21 February.

'Frank Taylor, of the *News Chronicle*, shouted something like "Aren't you talking to the poor blokes, then?" We went over to see him and he asked if we would like a beer and said a nurse would get some for us. Like ourselves, Frank did not know about the others.

'Before we left, I asked a nurse which hospital we should go to next, to see the other lads. She looked puzzled. I asked again where the other people were, and she said there were no others. She said the only survivors were in the hospital in which we were standing.

'That was when the whole thing really hit me. I was sickened and shattered. I just wanted to go home.

'Relatives and friends arrived and we began to be surrounded by newspapermen. I was asked if I would like to go back to the scene of the accident to help identify baggage, and I agreed.

'My bag was missing, but in the rack over my seat I found my briefcase and overcoat. In a pocket of the overcoat was a bottle of gin, a present from the British Embassy in Belgrade, still intact.

'And the pack of cards was still in my hip pocket, but a quarter inch was sliced off the top, cleanly, as if by a guillotine. That shows how close I came.

'I found a cap that belonged to Eddie Colman. The players used to go to a place called the Continental in Manchester, where, as a gimmick, the owner used to present flat caps with the person's name inscribed inside to mark a certain number of visits to his place.

'Eddie used to wear his cap, and there it was, in the wreckage. I also found a red and white scarf Eddie used to wear.

'The odd thing was that the baggage belonging to those who had died seemed to be intact. It was terribly upsetting reading all those labels. I found a briefcase that belonged to the United secretary, Walter Crickmer. It was filled with traveller's cheques. He also carried a silver hip-flask in it. It was still there, and Walter's wife gave it to me as a present when I took the briefcase back to her.

'By this time, Jimmy Murphy, the assistant manager, was in Munich. After a short time he decided it would be best if we went back home and got things moving again. The weekend match against Wolves had been cancelled, of course, but we were heavily committed with fixtures.

'We wouldn't go near a plane. We went by train and boat. And they upset me. Every time the train braked I went all tense and broke into a sweat. I was tense on the boat to Harwich, and the train to London was worst of all. It was fast, and every time it braked I was back in that plane again mentally.

'We didn't want to travel by train from London to Manchester. My wife, Teresa, and Harry's wife were in London. We were driven up in a big Rolls, and I was affected by that. Every time the driver braked at a corner or to stop at traffic lights, it was terrible.

'Teresa had missed the first news bulletin about the crash. When she heard the second bulletin it named the survivors, so, in a sense, she had the relief before she had the shock.'

Twenty-three people died as a result of their injuries in the Munich air disaster.

Eight of the victims were Manchester United players: Roger Byrne, Geoffrey Bent, Eddie Colman, Duncan Edwards, Mark Jones, David Pegg, Tommy Taylor and Liam Whelan.

Three were members of the club staff: secretary Walter Crickmer, trainer Tom Curry and coach Bert Whalley.

Eight were newspaper representatives: Alf Clarke, Don Davies, George Follows, Tom Jackson, Archie Ledbrooke, Henry Rose, Eric Thompson and Frank Swift.

2. The Making of a Legend

We're gonna rock, around, the clock tonight . . .

We were young then, when Bill Haley, with that kiss-curl plastered on the forehead of his moon face, blasted us into the era of rock 'n' roll. Suddenly, everything was fresh, new and exciting. Teenagers, hooked on the vibrations, were taking over the world, or so said parents and grandparents, conveniently forgetting their days of jitterbug and Charleston. There were Teddy boys, with Brylcreemed hair slicked up at the front and swept back into a D.A. (duck's rear) formation with long sideburns, and wearing lengthy, draped jackets with velvet collars, bootlace ties, drain-pipe trousers and crêpe-soled shoes.

In Hollywood, moody James Dean, with his frown, mumble and blue jeans, was the rebel without a cause, the symbol of a generation. It was a time for 'method' acting ('I *am* a tree') and Dean was beginning to out-Brando Marlon (*On the Waterfront*) Brando.

The frenzied beat of the music brought out the most primitive instincts in some. Haley's 'Rock Around the Clock' was the theme song of a film about school violence called *Blackboard Jungle*, and later became the title of a film featuring the rock 'n' roller himself with his backing group, the Comets. Cinemas all over Britain suffered damage as youngsters, carried away by the new sound, ripped out seats and generally ran riot.

Haley had a whole host of gyrating contemporaries. Elvis Presley, pelvis swinging, took a walk down Lonely Street to

25

'Heartbreak Hotel', Gene Vincent, curled round a microphone, mouthed 'Be Bop A Lula', and somehow we seemed to know what he was trying to say. Little Richard screamed at 'Long Tall Sally' and 'Lucille'. Jerry Lee Lewis had a 'Whole Lotta Shakin' Goin' On', and 'Goodness, Gracious, Great Balls of Fire!'

Tommy Steele, Britain's own star, sang 'Rock with the Caveman' at the "2I's" coffee bar in Soho, little Laurie London had the 'Whole World in His Hands' and Frankie Lymon and the Teenagers insisted 'I'm Not a Juvenile Delinquent'.

It was a mad, marvellous time; a relief in its contrast to the war-scarred 1940s. Life began to move slowly forward from an era of ration book austerity, the black market and 'making do' with what little was available.

Industrial towns had 'jam-butty' belts of closely knit, back-street communities, where small boys with woolly Balaclava helmets, urchin-grey pullovers and short trousers always too long for them, patched at the seat more often than not and held up by snake belts, kicked makeshift footballs. But we were moving towards a time when the more fortunate ones were buying 'Stanley Matthews' football boots from the Co-op. These were still rather inflexible, with cruelly solid toe-caps, far removed from the sophisticated slippers later introduced by the Continentals. But to possess 'Matthews' boots then was to have the winged feet of Mercury.

Footballs were still laced, heavy and bruising, and the professional game in England was insular, tending to run to fat on the complacency of a post-war attendance boom, though everyone was shaken in 1949 by the news that the Italian club Torino had been wiped out in an air crash at Turin.

In 1951, there was the Festival of Britain, and we stared in puzzled wonder at a giant metal cigar called Skylon and at the Dome of Discovery. But it was fun to sail on the Thames believing ourselves to be at the heart of the whole world.

That feeling intensified in Coronation year, 1953, when out came the Union Jacks and the bunting, all the schoolchildren received commemorative beakers from the Corporation and we crowded around twelve-inch television screens to watch the event, then celebrated with parties in the streets. That same year Everest was conquered, a feat which symbolized the 1950s, a decade in which our heroes, like Sir John Hunt and Doctor Roger Bannister, who in 1954 ran the first sub-four-minute mile in athletics, were respected rather than worshipped.

There was the sentimental tug of the 'Matthews Final', with Stanley dribbling and crossing from the right to help inspire Blackpool's fight back to beat forlorn, injury-weakened Bolton Wanderers 4–3. But during that year, 1953, the foundations of English football quaked under the impact of a tubby little Hungarian major and his revolutionary army.

It was shameful enough to have been beaten by the novices of the United States 1–0 in the 1950 World Cup, but that was in far-away Brazil and was shrugged off as a fluke that did not threaten our domain. Ferenc Puskas, the galloping major, and his cherry-shirted force, showed us the depth of our shortcomings by teaching us a lesson on our own sacred Wembley turf. Not only did the Hungarians become the first team from outside the British Isles to beat England on her own soil, they also opened our eyes to an entirely new concept of play.

Until then, a centre forward was generally accepted to be a strong, powerful, attacking player who would act as a human battering-ram against opposing defences, challenging forcefully on the ground and in the air and relying on wingers and inside forwards to run the ball on to his path to goal. The Hungarians had a new idea. Their number nine, Nandor Hidegkuti, played deep as the link man in midfield, creating openings for the probing, inventive front men, Puskas and Sandor Kocsis, and also surging forward to add additional power and surprise to their assaults.

Hidegkuti, and his telepathic wing half partner, Josef Bozsik, a member of the Hungarian House of Deputies, worked with such speed, accuracy and understanding that the deep-lying centre forward scored three of the Hungarian goals in their 6–3 victory.

When the Hungarians followed this triumph by beating England 7–1 in their own People's Stadium in Budapest, it was clear that there was an urgent need for rethinking and replanning. Perhaps the most important part of the lesson was that the English did not, after all, know it all and could no longer sit back looking down condescendingly upon those who had taken up 'our' game as mere jugglers with no shooting ability.

This was only the first phase of Puskas's influence on the game in Europe, for he was later to move to Spain following the Hungarian Uprising to become a member of the majestic Real Madrid team.

Manchester City adopted the Hungarian style, with Don Revie playing the part of Hidegkuti to Ken Barnes's Bozsik and Johnny Hart, Joe Hayes, Bobby Johnstone and Jack Dyson alternating as Puskas and Kocsis. It took them to Wembley in successive years, losing 3–1 to Newcastle United in 1955 (having been reduced to ten men when Jimmy Meadows had to go off with a knee injury that ended his career), and beating Birmingham City 3–1 in 1956.

But even before the Hungarians exposed England at international level, two men in particular were working towards the future. Stan Cullis, the manager of Wolverhampton Wanderers, one of the game's greatest centre halves and England captains, and Matt Busby, the manager of Manchester United, a former wing half of classical style and captain of Scotland, were harvesting the nation's richest potential talent.

Cullis and Busby worked in the belief that if a player was good enough, then he was old enough, building nurseries of young players and feeding them in a constant stream into first team football. The achievements of Wolves and United restored pride in English football, and the Continentals did not laugh for long.

United had won the FA Cup in 1948 and were runners-up for the League Championship four times before winning their first post-war title in 1952, with Jack Crompton in goal and men like John Aston, who would play anywhere, Johnny Carey, who almost played everywhere, Jimmy Delaney, a dazzling talent, Johnny Morris, the ball artist, Stan Pearson, the magnificent goal-taker, Jack Rowley, with the cannonball shot, and Henry Cockburn, a small but brilliant wing half.

Charlie Mitten, the cheeky winger, had left the club to follow his quest with the fortune hunters in Bogota, but Allenby Chilton was there to succeed Carey as captain, and, from the centre of the defence, he played a vital role in the dramatic change-over from experience to youth.

For three years from 1952, United's youngsters developed into a team able to dominate the First Division and ready to invade Europe. Johnny Berry was experienced, having been bought from Birmingham City, and Busby also spent to obtain goalkeeper Ray Wood (and later Harry Gregg) and centre forward Tommy Taylor to go with his Babes – Roger Byrne, Bill Foulkes, Eddie Colman, Mark Jones, Jackie Blanchflower, Duncan Edwards, Dennis Viollet, David Pegg, Geoff Bent, Colin Webster, Billy Whelan, Albert Scanlon, Wilf McGuinness, Bobby Charlton and Alex Dawson, with others constantly pushing their way to the top.

In 1955–6, they won the League Championship with sixty points, leaving Blackpool and Wolves gasping behind them with forty-nine points each. This breakthrough was made with enthusiastic, powerful, joyous football and was quickly acknowledged throughout the country.

It was not long before another disc became a part of the mid-fifties, along with the vibrant sounds of Haley, Presley and the rest. Borrowing the sunny, catchy rhythm of the Caribbean, the 'Manchester United Calypso' advised:

> . . . If they're playing in your town,
> Be sure to get to that football ground,
> If you do, then you will see,
> Football taught by Matt Busby;
> At Manchester . . . Manchester United,
> A bunch of bouncing, Busby Babes,
> They deserve to be knighted . . .

More than a decade later, Busby received a knighthood. Looking back with sadness and pride, he recalled those marvellous players who inspired another nickname: the 'Red Devils'.

'Ray Wood in goal. We bought Ray from Darlington for £6000. He was staid. You didn't get miracles from Ray. He was just there when it mattered, moving confidently into position and taking the ball cleanly.

'Harry Gregg, who cost us £23,000 from Doncaster later, was more of a showman in goal, and I am told he had a brilliant World Cup for Northern Ireland in Sweden in 1958. I didn't see it, of course, though I should have gone as Scotland's manager . . .

'There was Bill Foulkes, a big, rough, tough and reliable lad from St Helens, a no-nonsense right back, and later centre half, who played such a big part in the club's success. And Geoff Bent was emerging as the type of player who would have been regarded as a steady, dependable back.

'Roger Byrne at left back. An aristocratic footballer, majestic in his movement. Roger was so fast – one of the fastest full backs of all time – but at the same time he controlled his movement beautifully, like Nureyev.

'He would go up the wing to attack, but always had the speed to get back before the opposition could make anything of it. Often, he would give the other fellow a bit of a start before running to catch him, just to keep things interesting.

'Roger was brilliant at intercepting passes. He could read a situation very quickly and make a move to counteract it. And he had the knack of jockeying wingers into positions where he could tackle them before they could make a move.

'Great as they were, Stanley Matthews and Tom Finney never played well against Roger. In fact, I don't think Stan liked playing against him at all, though I always used to say in those days Stan used to play the Palladium. He always seemed to save his best for London.

'Eddie Colman at right half. Eddie, the little stylist with the wonderful shake of the hips and great control of the ball. Eddie was a beautiful player to watch, a contrast to Duncan Edwards but able to work perfectly alongside him. They complemented each other.

'Centre half was the one position we had not really sorted out, and we had two fine players in competition for the job. We always had competition for places in the first team, but centre half was probably most noticeable.

'There was Mark Jones, a big, commanding player. A strong type of centre half, dominating in the air. And there was Jackie Blanchflower, an astute player like his brother, Danny. Very skilful and, though not great in the air, very good just the same.

'Duncan Edwards. The player who had everything. He was so big, so strong and so confident. And so young.

'We used to look at players in training to see if we might have to get them to concentrate more on their kicking, perhaps, or their heading or ball control, whatever. We looked at Duncan, right at the start, and gave up trying to spot flaws in his game.

'Apart from anything else, he could move upfield and lash in goals when we needed them. John Charles was a giant of a player, a giant with great skill. But John and Duncan were different. Of the two, Duncan was the more powerful player. He used to move up the field, brushing players aside. Nothing could stop him and nothing unnerved him.

'The bigger the occasion, the better he liked it. He had no nerves before a game. He was like George Best in that respect. While other players would have to be pacing up and down a dressing-room, rubbing their legs, doing exercises and looking for ways to pass the time, Duncan, and George later, were always calm. They would just glance through a programme or get changed casually and wait without a trace of tension.

'I remember a game at Highbury, when I brought Ronnie Cope into the team and told Duncan, who was only a boy himself, to keep an eye on him. Believe me, you would have thought Duncan had been a professional for twenty years that day.

'He was a good type of lad, too. Even in those days, when football followers were not what they became later with regard to wanting to be with players socially, you still had people who waited for them. But Duncan did not want to know about the high life. He just wanted to play and go to his digs or go home. He lived for his football.

'We bought Johnny Berry from Birmingham for £25,000 in 1951 and he was a great little outside right. But it was something he did against United that prompted us to go for him.

'The season Portsmouth won the championship (1948–9) we were four points clear going into Easter, having still to play six games at home and four away. But we did a sort of Leeds United, losing to the bottom two clubs, Birmingham and Everton. Johnny scored a couple of goals against us and one of them was so well taken along the line it always stuck in my mind.

'Billy Whelan, had he been spared, would have been one of the greatest players of all time. He was a wonderful inside forward, tall, graceful and tremendously skilful. A slow kind of skill. But he was the opposite of Duncan Edwards. Billy had an inferiority complex.

'He was a terribly shy type of lad. I don't think he knew just how good he was. I remember one day when a section of the crowd were having a go at him and he just could not do a thing right. The following Tuesday I took him to one side and asked "What was wrong with you on Saturday?" He looked shy and awkward and said, very quietly, "Those people in the crowd were shouting at me". I looked at him and said, "If you're going to take notice of people like that you might as well go back home to Dublin right now".

'The next home game was against Wolves, and Billy scored a hat-trick. I'll always remember one of those goals in particular, when he took the ball into the penalty area and used his wonderful body swerve to dummy the defence this way, that way and every other way before sticking the ball in.

'Tommy Taylor was the player we needed to round the team off, to complete the picture – a big, strong finisher. We bought Tommy from Barnsley for £29,999 in 1953, knocking off the pound so he wouldn't be tagged a £30,000 player.

'Tommy was ideal. Brilliant in the air, so good that he would rank with the greats. Not only could he head for goal with great power, he could also turn in the air and head delicately to a man either behind him or alongside.

'He was also a great finisher with his feet, and an unselfish player. He wanted to score goals himself. Naturally, everyone does. But he really didn't mind who scored them as long as the ball went in. He was just as happy making goals for the others as scoring them himself.

'Dennis Viollet was the perfect match for Tommy. Dennis was quicksilver, a wonderful chance-taker. He would spot Tommy making a move for the ball, either in the air or on the ground, and could work out where to position himself to take advantage. He could read a situation before a defence could. And not only could he take chances, he could also create them with wonderful touches of skill.

'David Pegg was a great asset then and would always have been a great asset to any team because he was a natural left-flank player. David was very, very clever. He was our best left winger by a mile. Albert Scanlon was a good direct type of winger, but David was the kind you do not find very often.

'He was brilliant playing off another player. He knew just when to bring a team-mate into play and could vary his game.

Sometimes he would work the ball upfield with a team-mate and other times he would take men on himself. And when opponents were expecting him to do one or the other of those he would make a direct run and cross.

'David was affected by his game and if things were not going well for him he would take it to heart. But he could still overcome this because of his sheer talent.'

Those players were the cream of United, but the milk was also rich indeed: Bobby Charlton, Alex Dawson, Wilf McGuinness, Mark Pearson, Jeff Whitefoot, Ken Morgans, Colin Webster, Ronnie Cope, Johnny Giles, Nobby Stiles, Nobby Lawton, Johnny Doherty ... fighting for first team places and battling to keep places in the reserves.

The Football Association Youth Cup came to Old Trafford every year from 1953 to 1957 and the competition for places intensified, as Busby remembered:

'There were so many splendid players in the reserves, all fighting for first team places, that one season our average attendance figure for Central League matches was 11,000.

'Sometimes I would make as many as three changes at a time, but I always got stacks of letters from supporters, advising me who to put in and who to leave out. "What about Whelan?" they would write, and "Give McGuinness a chance" and "You can't leave out Charlton".

'All the players wanted to be in the first team, of course, and when one would start pressing his claims to me I would just say, "Look, son, you go out there on that green turf and show me that you are the best player and then I won't be able to keep you out of the first team".

'I wouldn't say I had problems, because we had a common understanding, though I suppose it's fair to speculate that a similar situation might have been more difficult later, with higher wages and percentages of transfer fees.

'At that time I felt I was in a position where I could have sat back for the next ten years while the team played. It was that good. I used to go to grounds hoping the other team would score an early goal to start us off and get us playing at our best.

'A lot of this might sound as if I'm just praising for the sake of it. Believe me, it is impossible to exaggerate about those players.'

When Busby walked into the United job in 1945, he had excellent players but a ground smashed by German bombers. He was a man obsessed by the need to build.

'People often ask when I decided that the most important job was to attract and develop young players. The answer is that the importance of young players was at the back of my mind from the day I arrived at Manchester City as a young player myself and was in digs with Jack Bray.

'I knew from my own experiences how lonely and insecure young players could feel and how much they needed a friendly smile, a word of encouragement and opportunities. I remember Alf Clarke, from the *Manchester Evening Chronicle*, calling to see me for my first interview after taking the job. With the ground in such a mess we were at Cornbrook Cold Storage, and I talked to Alf then about my plans to find young players.'

The man who 'signed' Busby for United was the late Louis Rocca, the club's chief scout. He wrote to Busby at the end of 1944, saying 'I have a great job for you if you are willing to take it on'. When Busby did take it on, Louis Rocca was the first of two famous Busby scouts.

'After Louis, a man respected as a judge of footballers and with a tremendous number of contacts, we had a little ferret called Joe Armstrong. On top of everything else, Joe had a way with people. He knew how to talk to the parents, how to reassure them.'

Shortly after his arrival at Old Trafford, Busby brought in Welshman Jimmy Murphy as assistant manager and chief coach, and the most famous partnership in football was born.

Backed by assistant coach Bert Whalley and trainers Tom Curry and Bill Inglis, they began to assemble and mould a wonderful youth team.

'Wolves and ourselves had similar ideas in those days,' said Busby. 'We were both keen to sign young players. We did not have the competition that we experienced later and, of course, the more the club gained a reputation for handling young players the more young players wanted to join us.

'Stan Cullis was not too pleased when we signed Duncan Edwards from Dudley, which was on Stan's doorstep. Joe Mercer, still playing for Arsenal at the time, was chatting to us about the current crop of boys and mentioned Duncan. We were also helped by the fact that Duncan wanted to play for United.'

A typical reaction to United's impact on the mid-fifties was expressed by Charles Buchan, former captain of England, Sunderland and Arsenal and widely acknowledged as one of the finest inside forwards of the 1920s. 'Manchester United's great achievements will always provide a topic for discussion. Much of the credit for their success goes to manager Matt Busby, who still trains with his players.

'Busby has not made the common mistake of trying to make his team play to a set plan. He treats each game as a separate occasion, calling for different treatment. This is Manchester United's great secret.

'On one occasion Matt told me, "You can never judge what the opposition is likely to do. Any plans should be based on the skill of your own players in adapting."

'That was the reason for Arsenal's success during the 1930s. The players were not restricted in any way. They pooled their brains in the interests of the side. And, like the Arsenal men, United's boys form part of a happy club.

'If they are dropped from the First Division side, they do not immediately ask for a transfer. They work harder than ever to win back a place in the team.

'There are some, like Irish international Jackie Blanch-flower and Wilf McGuinness, without a regular place, who are content to wait for their chance, knowing it will come. There can be no finer tribute to Matt Busby's shrewdness and tact than the discipline that prevails in United's ranks and the skill and harmony of the players.'

Busby's success with young players did not surprise those who had known him, like Cliff Lloyd.

Few men have influenced the social history of the game in England more than Lloyd, secretary of the Professional Footballers' Association, the players' advocate. He fought to give players greater financial security, more freedom of movement, wider powers of negotiation and the right to appeal in courts of football discipline.

Busby was an experienced, established star when Lloyd arrived at Liverpool in 1937 as a teenager, hoping to make the grade as a wing half but slightly unsure of himself.

'The maximum wage then was eight pounds a week and I was getting five pounds, which might not sound a lot but made me just about as well off as the players in the late 1960s and onwards when you consider the purchasing power of money then,' said Lloyd.

'You could buy a suit for fifty shillings, a three-bedroomed house for a few hundred pounds and a car for just more than a hundred pounds. And the average wage in industry was just over two pounds a week. Money had far more value in those days.

'I gave up a job driving a scooter around a cable factory at Helsby to have a go at professional football, and Matt impressed me right from the start. It was not just that he was such a fine wing half, relying on skill and playing it fair, with no time for the rough stuff. It was his whole attitude and appearance.

'If you had seen Matt walking to the ground you would never have taken him to be a player. He always had that marvellous bearing and, in a fawn overcoat and trilby, smoking his pipe, he looked more like a bank manager than a professional footballer.

'Matt was always the man young players would go to if they had any problems. Even then. He was always interested in the welfare of the younger players. He encouraged me a lot. And not just me. Everyone. I'd often play against him with Liverpool's Central League team in practice and he'd say things like "Good ball, Cliff".

'It never surprised me that he went on to do so well as a manager. To me, he always seemed destined for greatness.'

At the end of the war, when Busby went to Old Trafford, Lloyd continued his playing career with Fulham and then Bristol Rovers.

'But I always followed Matt's career closely. I remember standing behind one of the goals at Wembley in 1948, when United beat Blackpool 4–2 in the FA Cup Final.

'I may be detracting from certain people, but I've always believed that a team reflects its manager. Matt was a purist. He loved his players to express themselves.

'Perhaps I am in a minority in saying this, but I think coaching can have the wrong effect on players and eventually the game becomes strangled by coaching. Obviously, ability must be harnessed to the needs of a team, but it is possible to take coaching too far and stifle natural ability.

'Even when the game has flourished at youth level, a lot of the same youngsters have failed to come through the club system. It was never like that with Matt.'

In 1953, when the Babes were springing forth, Lloyd became secretary of the PFA and moved into an office at the Corn Exchange Building, behind Manchester Cathedral. (Billy Meredith, the legendary Welsh winger who played for both Manchester clubs, was in the chair when the Association was formed at the Imperial Hotel in 1907, but Lloyd, not famed as a player, was the man who made it truly effective.)

Lloyd's hectic days were lightened by visits to football

grounds to see the Babes. 'They had so many marvellous players, all so young. Boys playing in the first team and more boys fighting for places and more boys behind them and more boys joining the club,' he said.

'The big moan from players in England then, with the maximum wage and retain and transfer system in force,[1] was that they could too easily find themselves out of the first team, which meant losing bonus money, and unable to leave the club to try their luck elsewhere.

'Apart from anything else, players unable to win first team places were constantly in danger of becoming anonymous, complete unknowns. And that would make it harder to get a move, because other clubs would not know whether they were good or not, and harder to make an impression if they did get the chance, because of a loss of confidence.

'Matt had so many players at Old Trafford, and while that can be a lovely problem for a manager to have, it can also be a headache. He had a superb first team and fringe players like Wilf McGuinness, Freddie Goodwin, Jeff Whitefoot, Albert Scanlon, Ken Morgans and so on.

'He had to let some players go – players who could have walked into the team when the tragedy struck. But it was difficult at the time, with so many good players at the one club.

'Duncan Edwards was perfect then, young as he was, and it's hard to imagine how he would have developed with more experience on top of all that power and talent.

'I've never known anyone put forward Duncan as the greatest player of all time and get an argument about it, short as his career was. Matthews and Finney were around then, but even when their names are put forward as the greatest you will hear someone say "Yes, but . . ." That never seems to

1. There was then a limit laid down by the Football League as to how much players could earn and the rules provided for clubs to retain the services of players even after their contracts had expired, provided they paid a minimum of £8.50 during the playing season and £6.50 during the close season.

happen when Duncan's name is mentioned, even though he was a wing half and most of the candidates for the "all time great" seem to be forwards.'

The Babes were rich in talent and public acclaim, but their bank accounts were modest compared with those of players in the big time from the mid-sixties, when it was recognized that they were public entertainers with a limited career span.

Lloyd, a shrewd and determined worker, and the more publicized Jimmy Hill, led the fight to abolish the maximum wage and aided George Eastham in his courageous fight to free himself from Newcastle United. The players backed their union leaders with the threat of strike action, and the maximum wage was lifted for the 1961–2 season. It was not long before top club grounds needed parking facilities for the limousines of their footballers as well as their directors.

Earlier stars, including those of Busby's great teams of the forties and fifties, had to make do with the following maximum wages:

1946–7, £10 per week during the playing season, £7 10s during the close season

1947–8 to 1950–1, £12 during the season, £10 during the break

1951–2 to 1953–4, £14 and £10

1954–5 to 1956–7, £15 and £12

1957–8, £17 and £14

1958–9 to 1960–1, £20 and £17

1961–2, no maximum.

Fulham Chairman, Tommy Trinder, had said he wanted to pay England inside forward Johnny Haynes £100 a week. Now he could.

'It was typical of Matt that he should have backed the moves to remove the maximum wage,' said Lloyd. 'With so many top class players at United, he knew how serious the problem was. He wanted to reward his players realistically. But that was Matt. He always thought big and he always thought ahead. It took a big man to take his club into Europe against the advice of the administrators. When Chelsea won the League Championship, they declined the invitation to compete for the European Cup. When United became Champions the following year, Matt took the broader view. His move was progressive. Not only for United, but also for international football.

'We began to see styles of play that made us more aware of how the game was developing abroad and we could study, at club level, key players of national teams.'

There is no question that Cullis built a magnificent team, but it was Busby who created a legend.

3. Life as a Busby Babe

What was life like as a Busby Babe in those days when Manchester United seemed destined to dominate English and European club football?

Bill Foulkes recounted his steps from Whiston Boys Club to Old Trafford and the England team:

'I was a miner at Lea Green, near my home at St Helens, and was making fair progress in the job. After learning the ropes – literally – and spending some time on haulage down the pit, I went into the office as an assistant to the under-manager and was getting fifteen pounds a week.'

United spotted him in the usual way, a recommendation from someone who had seen him play locally followed by invitations to trials. 'I played a couple of trial games for a United selection team, one against St Bede's, but it was a while before the club contacted me and I started as an amateur and later signed part-time forms.

'Two things held me back from becoming a full-timer straight away. I liked the security the job at the colliery offered and I knew that if I left I would no longer be exempt and would have to go into the forces. So I was working and training and playing and generally doing a bit too much for my own good.

'I got flu and then had a series of boils on my face and cold sores. I was a bit of a mess. Matt saw me and said it was because I was getting too involved with everything and it would be better all round if I became a full-time professional.

'I said that would mean I would be called up, and I was twenty-two, while most of the lads doing National Service were only eighteen or so, but Matt didn't think it would. So I took the plunge and, sure enough, I began to feel better again. On the strength of becoming a full-time player I got married, but three weeks after the marriage and two weeks after becoming a full-timer, I was called up. The army fancied me for their team!

'I'll never forget the day I left. Duncan Edwards was called up at the same time. We were both first teamers then, in 1955, and I'd played for England.

'There was a rail strike, so we were picked up at the station and taken all the way to London in the back of an army truck. What a journey! There were no motorways then. When we got to London, I went one way, to move on to Blandford, Dorset, for my basic training, and Duncan went off somewhere else and was eventually stationed at Donington, near Shrewsbury. We had tears in our eyes when we parted that day. We were really sick about the whole thing.

'I arrived at Blandford and I'll never forget how hot it was. It was like a desert that year. I had only just arrived when United got in touch about a game at Birmingham on the Saturday and I said I'd be able to play. It was a daft thing to say, really, because there was no way I could get away. I hadn't got a pass.

'I climbed over the wall and went AWOL to Manchester. One of the lads at the camp was a Celtic supporter and he said he would cover for me as long as he could but I had to be sure to be back before Sunday morning.

'I got to Manchester and went with the team to Birmingham, where we drew 2–2, came back to Manchester with the team and then nipped to see my wife in Sale. She had arranged a taxi to pick me up to take me back to Manchester to catch the ten o'clock bus that would take the lads on leave back to their camps in the West Country.

'I only stayed an hour or so, but the taxi was late and I missed the bus. I stayed overnight and caught the Sunday night bus, but even though I was back at Blandford early

Monday morning I'd been found out. A corporal in my billet had told on me.

'When I was marched into the CO's office to explain why I had gone without a pass I said my wife had been ill. This was true. She had a spinal illness for a long time and we had been advised not to have children for four years because of this condition.

'When I said that, the CO offered me sick leave. But I said no, I would be all right ... until the following weekend. It was not long before they found out I was playing for United, and they were very good about it then.

'But I got back to camp after one match and the place was deserted. I asked where everyone was and was told: "They've been posted to Egypt". I felt sick, thinking I should have been with them, and started to look down the list of postings. But I was told: "You've been posted to Aldershot".

'It was great at Aldershot. A bit like a scene from the Sergeant Bilko television series. The CO was great. He wanted our battalion to win the Army Cup and I was put in charge of the team, played – and was chief scout! I don't think I've been fitter than during those days in the army.

'I was either training with the battalion, training the Boys' Corps, or training on my own. And when I wasn't training, I was playing. I never had any specific job, though I was supposed to be connected with transport.

'A captain advised me never to wear battle dress around the camp, but to go around in a track suit and pumps. He said if some of the sergeants caught me in battle dress they would make the most of it and try to make my life uncomfortable because I was a footballer.

'I took his advice. I never wore that battle dress. In fact when I came to leave, it was stuck to the door with mould. I was put in a special billet in a little room next to the canteen where the civilians who worked on the camp ate. It was great. John Little, who played for Rangers, shared the room with me for a while.

'No one ever knew where I was billeted. They knew I was on the camp, because I used to show my face from time to time and was always running around. But they didn't really know where to find me.

'The captain was happy enough, because I worked hard on his battalion team, which played on Wednesdays against semi-professional teams from the Hampshire League, and we reached the Army Cup semi-finals.

'As I say, I was tremendously fit. We had the usual public practice match at Old Trafford before the start of a season, with teams made up of a first team defence and a reserve attack against a reserve team defence and a first team attack, and for some reason Matt played Roger Byrne against me at outside left.

'Roger was fast. He used to frighten opposing wingers at left back with his speed. He didn't have to tackle them. He just had to show them that he was twice as fast as they were and they would be panicked into making a hasty pass.

'But he didn't get past me that day and Matt noticed because he said to me afterwards: "You've been doing a bit of running, haven't you?"

'We had some great times with the Army team on a tour of the forces on the Rhine. I was the captain and we had lads like Duncan, Eddie Colman, Maurice Setters, Peter Swan and Phil Woosnam in the team.

'But there was one trip we could have done without. We were going to play in Belgium and the journey was so rough – we travelled by sea in those days – that it would have taken a month before we could have walked on to a football pitch.

'I have never seen anyone as bad as Duncan was on that trip. The sea was tossing the boat all over the place and Duncan was lying on the floor. He was terribly sick, but couldn't get up off the floor. And we were all so bad that we were too ill to do anything to help him. When the boat lifted at one side, Duncan would roll along the floor, and when it lifted at the other side he would roll back again. This went on all the way across and by the end his uniform was not a pretty sight. Fortunately, when we arrived the game had been called off because the pitch was under water.

'Life was not always so funny. There was one officer who took an instant dislike to Duncan just because he was Duncan Edwards, a big lad and a star player while still so young. Duncan was not the kind of lad you would dislike usually. He used to keep himself to himself.

'This officer used to keep picking on Duncan. He was in charge of travel arrangements and he never gave Duncan any peace. He would pull him up over little things. Once, for instance, we were in a motor coach and it was terribly hot, but we were supposed to keep our collars buttoned and ties straight. Duncan was getting hotter and hotter and in the end he could stand it no longer and opened his collar and loosened his tie. He wasn't the only one, but the officer was at him straight away.

'It was the same when we were on our way to play Eintracht in Frankfurt. Pick, pick, pick. But this time Duncan had had enough and he had a go back. There was quite a row and it looked as if he wouldn't be allowed to play, but he made it in the end and we won 4–2.

'When you were in the army and playing professional football in those days, the club only paid you one pound a week and seven pounds if you played for them. But they were wonderful days in many ways.'

So were the days at Old Trafford.

'We had so many tremendous players, but when people talk about a team just going out there without any planning and playing pure football, they are not quite right. There was method in our play, but the instinctive element was there because we had so many intelligent players who knew what to do, where to move, how to find a team-mate and how to work all the angles. And there was a hardness in the side, too.

'I was at right back, and later moved to centre half, and

while I admit I was not one of the most skilful players around I was not as straightforward and orthodox as some people made me out to be.

'Roger Byrne was very fast, but was not a great tackler. As I've said, his speed frightened wingers and he had tremendous skill in forcing them into positions where it was difficult for them to make an effective move. He was a good captain, Roger, because he was a bit of a loner.

'Geoff Bent was emerging as a fine left back who could size up a situation and move in very quickly and effectively with his tackle. I'll always remember those long legs of his taking the ball away from a man.

'Eddie Colman was a wonderful player. Everyone talks about his body swerve, which was fantastic. He was so deceptive that he would have me going the wrong way, watching him from behind. But Eddie was very fast too. As fast as Roger Byrne. And his tackling was perfect, beautifully timed and giving away no free kicks, and he was a wonderfully accurate passer of the ball. Teams tended to underestimate Eddie because of his build – small and bulky – but they paid for it when they did. He was great fun, with an infectious sense of humour.

'Mark Jones was possibly the best man I've seen in the air. He wasn't particularly mobile, but was effective for all that. And even when I was at right back we operated naturally as a twin centre half cover. I used to clear more balls from the far post than Ray Wood and Mark put together. But that was because the team was so aware of situations.

'Jackie Blanchflower could play anywhere and would have been ideal as one of the modern midfield players. When I say that when Duncan was out and Jackie played left half he was marvellous, it gives you some idea of his ability.

'Duncan Edwards was incredible. Not only big and strong but beautifully balanced as well. Duncan could do everything. No one with any regard for their safety ever went into a tackle for a 50–50 ball with Duncan. Or any kind of tackle for that matter. There could only be one outcome. Duncan's sheer physical power would steam-roller opponents. They just couldn't withstand his strength. He was perfectly fair, but you just had to get out of his way.

'The best policy – as I found in practice games – was not to go in for the ball with Duncan but to try to get a toe in from the side and flick it away from him. He was not the greatest footballer in the air, but very, very good. He was a wonderful passer of the ball, with the ability to change the direction of a game with one move, and had superb delicate touches. His shooting ability had to be seen to be believed. He would have played on for a long time and it's rubbish to say he might have had weight problems later because he looked after himself well and would have trimmed down if necessary.

'Duncan was a serious, dedicated type of boy, but he was well aware of his ability and realized the value of money. He came from a quiet, ordinary background in Dudley, and knew that he had what it took to do very well for himself.

'Tommy Taylor would have been priceless in the 1970s as a "target man" because he was doing a similar job as United's centre forward in the mid-fifties. I have never seen a better header of a ball in attack, and though this was Tommy's main strength, he was also the best example you could have wished for of what is meant by strong, unselfish running.

'Dennis Viollet was a clever player then and became even better later when he played at centre forward.

'We have been able to see how Bobby Charlton developed and can only imagine how great the others would have been. There were class men there without question.

'There were a lot of players, but it was not too difficult to keep them happy because, financially, there was then only a matter of a couple of pounds' difference between playing for the first team and playing for the reserves. But competition for places was fierce and that was part of the overall power of the team.

'I was in at the start of the Babes and can remember the

big change-over coming at Huddersfield. Allenby Chilton had been going strong and Jack Rowley had been doing a great job at outside left, and though a few of the younger players were drafted in from time to time, it was at Huddersfield that the new United team began to take shape with a 2–2 draw. We won the League in 1956 and went into Europe the following season. We thought we were going to win the European Cup too.'

The Babes were growing in confidence and influencing all those around them.

Norman Bodell's name was then restricted to the lower division team-sheets of Rochdale, Crewe and Halifax. Later he became a Football Association coach in Zambia, manager at Barrow and coach at Wolves and Preston. He remembered his National Service days and a certain soldier: 'I was talking to this chubby little bloke up at Catterick Camp. Everything he wore was too big for him. His beret was too big, his denims were too big, even his boots were too big. He didn't look at all impressive and was saying "What a doddle I've got – regular rat catcher".

'We were talking for five or ten minutes before I realized who he was and said to myself, "God – it's little Colman". I was in the Seventh Royal Tanks, a physical training instructor, and Eddie was in the Signals. I think "rat catcher" was a job in name only. I don't think he did anything. He played for the army as well as United and he could have been in the sports stores as well. As an extra job I suppose they used to say "go and catch some rats".'

It was a time when professional footballers took National Service in their stride, as Norman recalled: 'We all knew we had to go in and that was that. I was up at Catterick from 1956 to 1958 and there must have been twenty-two players in our regiment. We would get passes to play for our clubs at weekends, and the facilities to keep in trim at the camp were excellent. Better than at the clubs in some cases.

'As a physical training instructor I was never away from

sport and the only thing I had against National Service was that I felt two years was just a bit too long. Otherwise I'm all for it because you learn self-discipline as well as many other things. I can always tell a lad who's done National Service but I think one year would have been enough then and that six months would be good for the lads today.

'Being at Rochdale meant that I was always near the hub of what was going on at United. The boys were marvellous. It was the best club side I've seen in this country – except perhaps Leeds United. They were all great, all wonder-boys, but big Duncan Edwards was exceptional. I once walked past him at Victoria Station, Manchester. We were both sixteen at the time and I was still at school. I was going to catch my train back home to Royton, near Rochdale, and Duncan was coming the other way, with his father I think. I remember saying to myself, "What the hell's this coming down here?" He was wearing a big overcoat and looked like a weight-lifter. He was frightening. It was amazing to contrast Colman and Edwards, two great players, one so small and the other a giant.

'But the most amazing thing to me was how the boys all came together, all such great players at the same club at the same time. It seemed to be fate. I know lots of lads like me used to think, "I should be one of them, playing for United", but when we'd seen them play we'd think "no way". And boys still go to United because of that legend.'

At the outbreak of rock 'n' roll, Jimmy Savile, disc-jockey, television personality, wrestler and dedicated charity worker, was the manager of Manchester's Plaza Ballroom, where the Babes were known to the local girls as the 'ten tall men' (perhaps one of them danced elsewhere).

'Yes, the Manchester United boys used to come to the Plaza,' he recalled. 'Some used to come to our lunchtime sessions, which were a new thing. You don't get them in this country now. I can remember seeing Oxford Street teeming with people when we charged threepence for two hours' dancing at lunchtime. There were great strictures all over town, from irate headmasters to irate football coaches, but the pull of my crumpet was stronger than the pull of their lessons and games. I used to say, "Make your school or training ground as attractive as my ballroom and I'll be fighting *you* for them".

'The United lads came mostly on Tuesdays and Sundays, particularly Sundays. We used to have a lot of private functions, sometimes three a week, and we'd always have a good sprinkling of football people and people from other sports as well.

'One player who used to come in – and I won't name him – used to just stand there with the rest. All the girls were dotty over the players and there was this very attractive girl who was obviously dotty on this player. So I said to her, "Why don't you go and claim him because he's a bit slow at coming forward?" She said, "Oh, I couldn't do that".

'"Well," I told her, "you're risking a lifetime of happiness and you are a lump of wood because I'm sure he fancies you. So what I'll do is this: I'll play this certain pop record and then put on a smooch record. Then I'll turn the lights down low and make it a ladies' invitation. And if you don't ask him to dance it's not worth talking to you."

'She went and stood close to the player in fear and trepidation, and when the smooch followed the pop song and the lights went down low and I announced a ladies' invitation, she launched herself upon him. And they were married a year later.

'People always say today is not like the old days, and they are usually the people who have got married and have kids and have big bellies. But I'm still in the business, still up to the hilt in it, and the days don't really change. The kids still enjoy themselves.

'But I can be objective about it. Those days in the fifties were great because you could play all sorts of music to the patrons and they would stand for real quality music. They would love Elvis and Bill Haley, but they would also like Vic Damone and Sarah Vaughan. These days they wouldn't know about such people. In the fifties they could tell you the names of all the stars and would know the words of all the songs. Now – apart from the top groups – people wouldn't recognize ninety per cent of those who play in any of the groups. They still have a good time, as I say, but not the same kind of good time.

'The Plaza at the time I remember was the social centre of Lancashire. In the dance-hall business the Plaza was considered the greatest in the country and I received the world's top dance-hall manager award from there.

'I remember it clearly because it was Bill Haley's first time at the Odeon, next door, and ninety per cent of the shops in Oxford Street had their windows boarded up or had minders guarding them. People talk about football hooligans today, but that's what it was like then.

'Oxford Street was filled with lads with long jackets and suede shoes. A girl from the university got into the Odeon manager's bathroom, where Bill Haley had taken a bath, and filled a medicine bottle with Bill's bathwater which she drank in public the next day as part of a rag-week stunt. Manchester had some of the greatest characters in those days and even though I have fantastic times today and the kids do, too, I think those were the best days.

'The fifties were the start of the generation gap, when adults began to flounder in a psychological, psychedelic abyss. Whatever came after were just branches of the tree – the trunk of it all grew in the fifties.

'After the years of war and of deprivation there was the great awakening, with luxuries like holidays. In those days I went on holiday to the south of France, and it was such a big thing that I stuck a big sign, twelve feet by twelve feet, outside the place with the announcement "Jimmy Savile is going to the south of France, leaving your entertainment in the very capable hands of his good friends". Everything was new and exciting then and I suppose we were wonderfully naïve. Now it's "seen it all before" and the attitude is more blasé.

'I personally have never been to a football match in my life, firstly because I was never able to go when I was able to go, if you follow my meaning, and secondly because if I went now I'd be murdered by 50,000 people jumping on my head, because everybody knows me. But I admit I am now a television football watcher of "my teams". They are Manchester United, of course, Leeds United and Bournemouth, where I have a big entertainments complex which is often visited by some of the Bournemouth players.

'Those Manchester United players who came to the Plaza were all model lads. We never had anything even remotely resembling trouble. They were all like the player I mentioned earlier – the one I married off! – quiet and incredibly attractive to the girls because they were so quiet and retiring.

'The players of today, just like the teenagers of today, are more self-assertive. In those days, those of us with money were very conscious of those who were without. We used to play it very cool. Today you might get a player whose club have paid £300,000 for him. It's part of his gimmick. Everybody else knows about it. The days of being shy about having money are over. There's nothing wrong in that. It's just another example of the way times change.'

Manchester's most popular night club of the period was the Cromford, off Market Street, where Paddy McGrath frequently played host to the Babes. McGrath, who was later to extend the image of American Hugh Hefner to the northwest of England with Playboy of Manchester, was more than an entertainer of United's famous sons. He was also one of the club's staunchest supporters.

'I supported United before those kids were born,' he said. 'I've watched them since the 1920s . . . and they never had a side before Matt came to a bomb site and took over a team of lads with talent and moulded them by switching one player here, another there and so on.

'During the war I was a physical training instructor with the RAF at Heaton Park and used to run the football teams. Heaton Park was an embarkation centre, and United's Louis Rocca and other club scouts used to call to ask "Have you any professionals in the camp?" We often had, and would let the clubs have them when we could so they could keep going.

'The Cromford was a members' club, opened in 1954, and became a great meeting place for sportsmen, particularly footballers and boxers. We used to have the big race call-overs and often held weigh-ins for the boxing at Belle Vue.

'Those United players were great lads and mixed very well. They often came in for lunch during the week and at weekends they would gather with their wives and girlfriends. One or two held their wedding receptions at the Cromford, including Roger Byrne and Johnny Doherty.

'I suppose one of the main reasons why they were all so close and mixed well socially was that they were nearly all of an age. Apart from Johnny Berry, who had been in the game longer, they were in their teens or early twenties. They all grew up together at United, whereas later, when lads like Denis Law were at the club, married and with a few children, the age groups were different. And so were the tastes. The younger lads might like discos, while others would prefer to go out for a meal, and so on.

'When Matt arrived, United never looked back, and the team he had in the fifties was so good that I reckon it would have ended up like the Harlem Globetrotters basketball circus – so much in a class of its own that it would have had to play exhibition games.

'The blend was terrific, for England as well as United. Just think of Duncan Edwards – his shirt was better than some of the players who came into the game later. If you'd put Duncan's shirt on a line at Old Trafford, 50,000 would go to watch it. He was in a different class.'

4. 1956–8

In the season of 1956–7, United attempted the 'treble', a target not even dreamed of before. As well as defending the League Championship and challenging for the FA Cup, they became the first English club to accept an invitation to compete in the European Cup, a competition founded by 'L'Equipe', the French sports paper.

The season before, Chelsea had turned down an invitation to join the great European adventure on the advice of the Football League Management Committee. Stressing that the English League programme was above all other considerations and that there were enough fixtures in a domestic season without adding to them, the Management Committee tried to discourage United from committing themselves to Europe. But Busby, believing European competition to be the next logical step in the progress of the game and confident he had the playing resources to take him through the additional fixtures, made the move that changed the course of soccer thereafter.

He was vindicated in less than nine months, by which time United had again won the League Championship, had reached the FA Cup Final and had become European Cup semi-finalists.

The world began to take notice of the Babes as soon as word spread of their result in the first round of the European Cup. They were drawn against Anderlecht, of Belgium, and won the first leg of the two-match tie 2–0 in Brussels.

That was nothing compared with what followed on a rainy night at Maine Road, Manchester (Old Trafford was still without floodlighting) when the Babes touched form that was scarcely credible, to win 10–0 with four goals from Viollet, three from Taylor, two from Whelan and one from Berry. And everyone tried tremendously hard to add Pegg's name to the scoreline.

In the second round, United had a tougher time against West Germans, Borussia Dortmund, winning the first leg 3–2 at Maine Road and hanging on with a goalless draw in Germany.

Then came Bilbao in the third round, with United drawn away for the first leg of the tie on a night that stuck in Busby's memory: 'The conditions were dreadful, a combination of mud and slush following heavy rain and snow. We went 3–0 down, but pulled back to 3–2 and, with the second leg to come, I didn't think that was too bad.

'But Bilbao went and scored another two goals, silly goals, and we looked to be in real trouble, three goals behind again. Then Billy Whelan got the ball in his own half and started to move through the mud and slush. Well, not so much move as meander. He seemed to be going so terribly slowly, beating this man, then that man, and meandering on. I wondered when he was going to release the ball, but he just went on and on and on, beating more and more men. Finally, he reached the penalty area and we all waited for him to shoot. But he was still taking his time and he had that defence in a rare tangle before scoring a brilliant goal to make it 5–3. And, of course, we managed to win a tremendously exciting second leg to go through on aggregate.'

But next morning, when United were due to fly home from Bilbao, there was an ominous scene at the airport. It had been snowing all night and the two aircraft that had brought the team and officials were frost-bound. United had to return home to play a League game against Sheffield Wednesday, and, knowing how the League Management Committee had viewed their entry into Europe, everyone in the party pitched in to clear the snow from the two aircraft.

Players, officials, pressmen, supporters and airport staff went to work and finally the planes were fit for take-off and returned to London.

There was terrific excitement at Maine Road for the second leg, in which United scored, had two more 'goals' disallowed and finally won 3–0 to go through on aggregate, 6–5.

United were in the semi-finals, ready to meet the holders, Real Madrid, who had beaten Rheims 5–3 in Paris the previous year to win the first tournament from an entry of eighteen. There was an entry of eighteen again in 1956–7, when United began to feel invincible but were, in the words of Bill Foulkes, 'about to be shown that we still had some way to go and were not as good as we thought we were'.

Foulkes recalled those semi-final matches against Real:

'Matt had been to watch Madrid and was full of them when he talked to us before we played them in the semi-final. You could tell he admired them from the way he kept saying "great" this and "great" that and building up their players, unwittingly, I'm sure – he was just so impressed by their ability and style. I remember his turning to me and talking about a left winger called Gento, saying "He can run, Bill, he can run".'

In the Chamartin Santiago Bernabeu Stadium, 130,000 spectators awaited United.

'We were soon to realize the boss was not exaggerating, though we played well even though we lost 3–1 in Madrid. Gento could run all right – and do so many other things as well. He was particularly good at positioning himself to receive the ball and once he got it, he would go.

'I thought I played him fairly well, even though I never touched the ball. I simply tried to cut off all the angles and jockey him into positions where he would not be so effective. But it was difficult because he had wonderful service from Rial, who could ping the ball from all angles.

'Their defence didn't look so great that day, though. They were frightened of Tommy Taylor, who was getting up to everything in the air. The only way they could contain Tommy was to use methods they would never get away with today. They would grab him around the waist or hang on to his shoulders. Not just one of them, but two or three. Anything to keep him away from the ball.

'I've never seen anything quite like Di Stefano. He was their general and had so much ability and knew everything there is to know about the game. He controlled everything and could play everywhere. I am told he was even great in goal.

'But during that game in Madrid, Jackie Blanchflower beat him once with a superb flowing movement, taking the ball from Di Stefano, turning stylishly and pushing away a great ball. Di Stefano was upset. It obviously didn't happen to him very often, and he reacted by kicking Jackie on the backs of his legs. I moved in then and shoved Di Stefano in the back to let him know I wasn't having any of that. He held up his hands, nodded, said "Foulk-es" in an apologetic way, and we got on with the game.

'The big lesson came in the return match at Old Trafford (the floodlighting had now been completed). We drew 2–2 but they played us off the park. They were absolutely brilliant, stroking the ball around perfectly. We gained a lot from the experience of playing against them then.'

So, on 25 April, United were out of Europe and Madrid went on to retain the trophy in their home city with a 2–0 win against Fiorentina. But though the 'treble' dream had ended, United seemed certain to end the season with the League Championship–FA Cup double as they prepared to meet Aston Villa – then the last club to achieve the double, in 1897 – at Wembley on 4 May.

United arrived at Wembley as League Champions with 64 points, ahead of Tottenham Hotspur and Preston, both with 56 points. Busby's team to attempt to clinch the double was: Ray Wood; Bill Foulkes, Roger Byrne; Eddie Colman, Jackie

Blanchflower, Duncan Edwards; Johnny Berry, Liam Whelan, Tommy Taylor, Bobby Charlton and David Pegg.

But United lost goalkeeper Wood within six minutes. He was carried off the field with a smashed cheekbone and concussion after being charged by Aston Villa winger Peter McParland. Substitutions were not allowed, so Jackie Blanch-flower took over in goal. He made some splendid saves, too. Wood, still dazed, came back on to the field in the second half and made a game effort to contribute something from the wing and though Taylor headed a glorious goal and Wood went back into goal near the end, Villa won 2–1, with McParland scoring both goals.

Only one of the three trophies went to Old Trafford, but there was an interesting postscript to the FA Cup Final, as Cliff Lloyd recalled: 'When United played Villa at Old Trafford in the Charity Shield we all wondered what would happen, because there was still some bad feeling about McParland's charge of the goalkeeper. We didn't have to wait long, because Wood and McParland met in the centre circle and shook hands as captains for the day, and that was the end of the matter. A master stroke. Matt knew a gesture like that could only help matters and ease the tension. He always was a diplomat.'

Wolverhampton Wanderers came through strongly to lead the First Division table at the start of the 1957–8 season and, after critical eyes had wondered if the hectic pace of the previous season was beginning to react against them, United began to make progress in the FA Cup and European Cup.

The third round of the FA Cup took them to Workington, where they lost an early goal but soared through on the strength of a brilliant hat-trick by Dennis Viollet in an eight-minute spell during the second half. United then beat Ipswich 2–0 in the fourth round.

In the European Cup, victories over Shamrock Rovers, of Dublin (6–0 and 3–2) and Dukla, Prague (3–0 and 0–1) put them through to the quarter-final games against Red Star, Belgrade. And they won the first leg of the tie 2–1 at Old Trafford, with goals by Charlton and Colman.

Eric Cooper, former Sports Editor of the *Daily Express*, remembered a visit to Burnden Park, Bolton: 'It was mid-week, shortly before United left to play Arsenal at Highbury (winning an epic, 5–4) and then went on to Belgrade.

'They took time off to watch Bolton Wanderers beat York City in an FA Cup replay. The ground was full, and manager Bill Ridding arranged for left-over VIPs and journalists to be put in the paddock. So there I was, with the United lads, just near the players' exit.

'We saw Terry Alcock, deputizing for Nat Lofthouse, score three goals for Bolton. Terry was a fine player but was never really taken to heart by the Bolton fans because, unlike Nat, he didn't head goals from a yard above the crossbar. Terry later went on to do well for Norwich.

'It was a truly happy crowd in that paddock. Mark Jones, in his pork-pie hat, was celebrating a return to the centre half spot he had regained after a long spell. He had taken over again from Jackie Blanchflower about three or four weeks earlier. Matt Busby had also at this time dropped Johnny Berry, Billy Whelan and David Pegg and brought in Ken Morgans, Albert Scanlon and Bobby Charlton. This was when Charlton had just begun to have a regular place in the first team.

'David Pegg was philosophical about it that day at Bolton. "I'll just have to play harder to get my place back," he said. David had just taken up pipe smoking and had a brand new pipe with him. He was sucking at it all the time, but there was no tobacco in it. Everyone was ribbing him about it. I never did know whether he ever really smoked that pipe.'

On 5 February 1958, Henry Rose filed his last match report to the *Daily Express* from Belgrade. His rating of the game was three stars out of a possible five, and he wrote:

Red Star 3, Manchester United 3
(Aggregate: United won 5–4)

'Manchester United survived the Battle of Belgrade here this afternoon and added another shining page to their glittering history by drawing 3–3 with Red Star and winning the two-leg tie 5–4. Now they go into the semi-final of the European Cup for the second season in succession after a rough-tough match of inflamed tempers and crazy refereeing.

'Every ounce of spirit was wrung from their brave hearts in an almost unbearably exciting second half. In that half, despite their first-half lead of 3–0, they were forced through injuries to Duncan Edwards (ankle) and Ken Morgans (thigh) to fight a magnificent rearguard action until the final hectic seconds. They had to fight not only eleven desperate footballers and a fiercely partisan 52,000 crowd, but some decisions of Austrian referee Karl Kainer that were double-Dutch to me. I have never witnessed such a one-sided exhibition by any official at home or abroad.

'United gave a sweet and rhythmic display of all the arts and crafts of soccer in the first half that made you proud to be British. They showed versatility in the second half by a display of tough tackling, but the tally of twenty-four free kicks for fouls against them as against eleven against Red Star was completely out of focus.

'The crazy climax to Herr Kainer's interpretations, which helped to inflame the crowd against United, came in the fifty-fifth minute when he gave a penalty against Foulkes, United's star defender. Nothing is wrong with my eyesight – and Foulkes confirmed what I saw ... that a Red Star player slipped and pulled the United back down with him. A joke of a ruling it would have been had not Tasic scored from the spot. I found it easy to forgive Edwards for protesting against a free kick against Colman for a perfectly fair tackle.

'Edwards had his number taken by the referee.

'"As great a performance as ever I have seen from our lads," was the verdict of delighted Matt Busby. Over the piece he could be right, but one would have to stretch a point and make allowances for some hefty tackles that should have no place in the armoury of his talented team and if the fact can be forgotten that United had two gift goals. Only ninety seconds had ticked off when centre half Spajic fluffed a clearance. The ball hit Taylor, rebounded to Viollet, who scored.

'Morgans was *kicked* on the thigh, Edwards in the ankle. But the rhythm down the middle was not upset.

'Charlton had what looked like a *perfect goal* from Scanlon's corner *disallowed* in the fourteenth minute, and just as this excited crowd were beginning to spring into violent vocal action they were silenced by two goals from Charlton in three minutes. They were a left-foot drive in the twenty-eighth minute and a right footer in the thirty-first as right back Tomic all but boobed his clearance from Edwards' centre.

'It was 3–0 (or 5–1) and, it seemed, all over bar the shouting.

'But two minutes after half time Kostic scored with a twenty-yarder.

'Then the fantastic penalty from which Tasic scored.

'Could the gallant United defence hold out against some magnificent, mazy football?

'Gregg was *hurt*, Morgans and Edwards were *limping*; Byrne was *warned for wasting time*. United players were *penalized* for harmless-looking tackles.

'I thought Herr Kainer would have given a free kick against United when one of the ball-boys fell on his backside.

'*Sheer agony.* There were only palpitating seconds to go. United lined up for a free kick, awarded against Gregg for handling the ball outside the penalty area. Kostic's shot hit Viollet's head and the leaping Gregg could only palm the ball into the net – a fantastic recovery by Red Star.

'The ball is hovering dangerously in the United penalty area. Left wing Scanlon seizes the ball, blazes a wild kick upfield ... anywhere ... who cares? ... the danger is over. Comes the final whistle and United are through.

'*Heroes all.* None greater than Billy Foulkes. None greater than Bobby Charlton, who has now scored twelve goals in the eleven games he has played since he went into the side at inside right on 21 December. But all eleven played a noble part in this memorable battle.

'*Individual rating*: Gregg 4 stars; Foulkes 5, Byrne 4; Colman 4, Jones 4, Edwards (hurt) 3; Morgans (hurt) 3, Charlton 5, Taylor 4, Viollet 3, Scanlon 3.'

Early the following evening in Manchester, there was a news flash on television: 'A report from Germany says that the plane, an Elizabethan, carrying the Manchester United football team and officials and journalists crashed on take-off at Munich. We will bring you more news later.'

More news later ...

Anne Gilliland, aged fourteen, was on her way home from The Hollies Grammar School, Fallowfield, when a neighbour told her about the crash.

'This particular neighbour often used to kid me when United had lost and I got very annoyed with her when she told me about the crash because I thought she was kidding again. But she said it was not the sort of thing she would joke about, so I dashed off to get a newspaper,' recalled Anne.

'There was nothing in the headlines and I began to wonder what was going on until I saw the stop press – "United plane crash ... Many dead". I cried and cried until I could not speak. When I got home my dad put on the radio and we listened for more news coming through.

'I was sobbing so much that I was close to becoming hysterical. No one could do anything with me. I was waiting for news about Roger Byrne, my big favourite in the team. There had been no news about him and I was clinging on to that as a little thread of hope. But news of Roger's death came later that night. I went to bed, but I could not sleep.'

Chris Fiddler, another fourteen-year-old, arrived home from Salford Grammar School in time for the news flash on television. 'There were no names and I just hoped for the best,' he said. 'I think I had already begun to accept that some of the players must have been killed before the details started to come through later. I stayed up late, and I cried.'

Jimmy Savile had been preparing for that night's Manchester Press Ball at the Plaza. 'I put a notice outside the Plaza. It just said, "Press Ball cancelled". Then I locked the door and we sat around, my staff and myself, listening to reports as they came through on the radio. We had to put the radio in the middle of the floor before it would work properly – something to do with the aerial. All around there was food prepared for the guests and though we were in a ballroom, dancing was the furthest thing from our minds.

'Even as we heard the news bulletins it was hard to conceive that such a terrible thing had happened. We stayed there all night. It was one of the most shattering experiences ever to confront a city – the biggest disaster Manchester had ever known.'

Next day Manchester was still unable to accept what had happened to her sons. The place was numbed with horror and sorrow. Already a shop in Sale, Cheshire, had sold out of black ties.

'The silence was unbelievable on the bus to school,' said Anne Gilliland. 'I sat there with my red and white scarf around my neck and cried my way to school. Everyone I saw looked stunned.

'I used to get into a lot of trouble at school because of my interest in football. It was taboo and the attitude was that young ladies did not go to football matches. I had been watching United for two years. My father was a Manchester City fan, but he let me go to watch United when I was twelve.

I went all over the country watching them. I also went to watch Roger Byrne's wedding.

'That day after the crash I felt as if I had lost all my relatives at once. My school was strict about uniform and although sometimes I used to wear my United scarf hidden underneath my coat, that day it was around my neck for everyone to see. I was going to be defiant and not make any secret of my feelings. But the attitude at school had changed and prayers for the players were said at assembly.'

Chris Fiddler had only a short distance to travel to school, 'but I could sense the shock everyone felt. All the boys at school were United supporters and when I arrived everyone was talking about the crash, including the teachers. With being at school I couldn't afford to travel to see the team, but I used to go to all the home matches.'

Everyone lost something at the end of that runway in Munich. Some lost everything.

While Matt Busby was fighting for his life under the care of Professor George Maurer, Chief Surgeon at the Rechts der Isar Hospital, United had already lost three men vital to their organization, secretary Walter Crickmer, assistant coach Bert Whalley and trainer Tom Curry.

Walter Crickmer was the club's longest serving official. He had been at Old Trafford for twenty-eight years, the last twenty-one years as secretary, and had been awarded the Football League's Gold Medal for long service.

Bert Whalley, a former United centre half, had been forced to retire as a player in 1948 because of an eye injury. He had been with the club for twenty years and was in charge of the young players, a quiet, studious type and a guiding hand behind the successful Youth Cup team.

Tom Curry had played for Newcastle United from 1911 to 1928, when he joined Stockport County. He became trainer at Carlisle United and moved to Old Trafford from there in 1934. His dedication was such that he would bring his open razor to the ground so that he would not waste time shaving at home. He was a Church of England man, and whenever United were away from home on a Sunday he would tell the players, whatever their persuasion: 'Don't forget to get along to the service.'

Those men helped shape the careers of players whose names will live for ever.

5. Geoffrey Bent

'*Geoffrey Bent was my personal friend and was always recognized within the club as probably the best player who could not get into the first team. He could not nudge out Roger Byrne, the best left back in the country, but would have walked into any other First Division team.*'

IAN GREAVES

A footballer on crutches arrived at Stretford Memorial Hospital to visit a patient and the nurses helped him to the ward upstairs, gathered around the bed and generally made a fuss. This was September 1957, and Geoffrey Bent's wife, Marion, had presented him with a daughter, Karen.

Geoffrey's right foot was in plaster, recovering from a second break during his career with Manchester United. The split bone had been plugged at St Joseph's Hospital, but it would take more than an injury to keep Geoffrey from his wife and darling daughter. When the plaster was removed, Geoffrey was able to wheel Karen in her pram up King's Road, Chorlton. He was delighted with himself.

A month before Christmas he went to United team-mate Eddie Colman's twenty-first birthday party, but half-way through the evening he left the celebration and popped home to check that Marion and Karen were safe and well. He was that kind of man.

The New Year, 1958, began with United out of the chase for the League Championship but challenging for the FA Cup and the European Cup. At twenty-five Geoffrey was understudy to left full back Roger Byrne, United's captain and an England international, and his scope was limited.

By early February, Geoffrey had fully recovered from his injury and was playing well. United were due to go to Belgrade. Defender Ronnie Cope thought he would travel with the team as first reserve, but Roger Byrne had an ankle injury and on the Sunday, the day before the party left, Geoffrey was told he would be joining them as reserve. He said to Marion: 'I don't know why they're taking me, because I'm sure Roger will be fit.'

On that Sunday, a neighbour was busy decorating and Geoffrey teased him, saying: 'Oh, I see your wife's locked you in the room until you've got that job finished.'

'Well,' said the neighbour, 'at least I'll still be asleep in bed when you're going off with United in the morning.'

The pair were often playing jokes on each other. In fact, during the Christmas past, the neighbour had poked a flute through Geoffrey's letter box and awakened the household with a high-pitched tune. Geoffrey decided it was his turn now and, after saying his farewells to Marion and five-month-old Karen, he left the house, tip-toed over to the neighbour's, hammered on the door until there were sounds of awakening inside, then slipped across the road into the morning mist.

The neighbour knew who had disturbed his morning slumbers but he did not get a chance to play another trick in return.

'Geoff didn't like flying. He used to get nose bleeds and also had to put drops in his ears,' remembered Marion, who has since remarried and divorced. She is now called Mrs Ridgway, but said: 'Karen and I have been on our own for twelve years now. Karen calls herself Bent and I intend to change my name back again.'

Marion, a clerk in the finance department of Home Help at Worsley and living at her mother's home in Eccles, looked through a photograph album and picked out a picture of a fair-haired boy of two-and-a-half years standing on a chair.

'That's Geoff outside his house,' she said, and smiled. 'Look at those little boots he's wearing. His mother had a thing about boots – she always used to say "Boots will give you firm ankles". She said the same to Karen.'

Mother, Mrs Clara Bent, died in November 1972, but Geoffrey's father, Clifford, a retired miner of seventy-one, is still alive and lives at Little Hulton, near Bolton.

Home to Geoffrey, an only child, was Irlams-o'-th'-Height, on the outskirts of Swinton.

'Geoff's house was at the back of some shops,' said Marion. 'It didn't have a front door or a back door. The only way in was down a side entry and you had to duck your head to get through the door.

'But the first thing you saw when you went in was a sign that said "Home Sweet Home" and that's just what it was. Humble but homely. They had a big black grate, and the stairs were in the living room. When you went upstairs you turned into Geoff's mother's room and you had to go through this room to get to Geoff's room.

'Geoff's mum used to keep the place spotless. There would always be a snow-white tablecloth spread on the table, but sometimes, when there was a sudden gust of wind outside, smoke would be blown out from under the grate and the cloth would be covered with bits of soot. Geoff's mum would just gather up the cloth, take out another, also snow-white, spread that one in its place and carry on as normal.

'We used to joke that you needed a bus service to the toilet, which was outside. And if you wanted a bath, there was a big tin one on a hook in the kitchen and you just put it in front of the fire, filled it up with water and there you were.

'Bonfire Nights were always marvellous round there, a real treat, and Geoff used to get fireworks from his mum and dad right up to the time we were married.'

Geoffrey went to St John's Junior School, where he won a scholarship to Tootal Road Grammar School. 'His mum used to see he did his homework before he went out,' said father, a washer who had worked on the rail trucks at Sandhole Colliery for fifty years.

'I'd sooner have rugby than soccer,' his father declared. 'I always used to follow Swinton, right from when they had the old Chorley Road ground, and a cousin of mine, Jimmy Grice, used to play in the same team as people like Nobby Smith, Jack Bailey and Harold Worsley. It wasn't a great team, but it got better.

'Geoff wouldn't play rugby, even though one of his teachers wanted him to play. It was always soccer with Geoff.'

He did find time to join the Boy Scouts and, later, the Boys' Brigade, and he was a strong swimmer, with a life-saving certificate to prove it. In fact, Geoffrey's first medal was not awarded to him for football, but for rescuing a boy from Salford Canal.

That was in 1946, when Geoffrey was thirteen, and the medal was presented by the 'Humane Society for the Hundred of Salford'. It is now at his father's home, along with the medal he won a year later as captain of the Salford Boys soccer team, winners of the English Schools' Trophy.

The ball used in the second leg of the final, against Leicester Boys, at Old Trafford, on 7 June 1947, its T-panelled leather well polished, stands on father's sideboard, atop a silver cup won by Geoffrey's grandfather, Isaac – one of five that athlete Isaac picked up for running, all on the same day.

There are other medals and photographs on the sideboard, and on a wall is a framed caricature of Geoffrey as captain of Salford Boys. On top of his father's television set is a small lamp, the shade of which is covered with the names of United's great players of the 1950s.

'At school Geoff played inside left. He later played at half back and then, later still, moved to left back,' his father recounted, adding: 'Apart from Salford Boys, Geoff also played for Barton Villa in the Eccles and District League.

'I'm only five feet five-and-a-half inches myself, and Geoff was on the small side at school. But he was five feet eleven-and-a-half inches when he was with United.'

Marion had Geoffrey's home-made scrapbook, a collection of newspaper cuttings recording the triumph of Salford Boys, including, in pride of place, Geoffrey pictured with Frank Swift at a special presentation party.

Marion met Geoffrey when she was nineteen and he seventeen. 'He had been dating my younger sister, Betty, for about three weeks, but I didn't take much notice of him at first,' she said.

'Then one night he was in the house when I was ready to go out dancing. "Can anybody come?" he asked, and I smiled and said "Of course". And I thought "he's a bit of all right".

'It wasn't long before Betty and Geoff split up. They were not really suited. Betty is full of beans but Geoff was more on the quiet side then. One night I was at Swinton Palais and Geoffrey asked me to dance. He said, "The lads I'm with think I'm a bit cheeky to ask you to dance after taking your sister out".

'"It's a free place," I said.

'"Well, would you think I was cheeky if I asked to take you out?" he said. And that's how we got together. We were married in 1953, when I was twenty-three and Geoff twenty-one, and went to live in King's Road.'

Before he signed full-time professional forms for Manchester United, Geoffrey completed his apprenticeship as a joiner with a Salford firm. 'Duncan Edwards worked at the same place. United had put them there to learn a trade but Duncan was not very interested in joinery. He didn't think about anything else but football. The lads used to kid Duncan about his brains being in his boots, but he was a wonderful person.'

Geoffrey was on good terms with all the players at Old Trafford, his particular friends being Ian Greaves, Bryce Fulton, Tom McNulty, Eddie Lewis, Colin Webster, Mark Jones and Ronnie Cope.

'I used to go to the matches occasionally with the wife of one of Geoff's friends,' said Marion. 'I didn't tell Geoff I was going because he would only have said "Why are you going to watch when you don't know anything about it?"

'I'd tell him when he came home and more often than not I'd start going on about Duncan Edwards. I'd say things like "That Duncan Edwards is a fantastic player". I think Geoff got a bit tired of hearing it after a while.

'I didn't go to the game against Bilbao at Maine Road, but I didn't have to because we could hear all the noise from King's Road. Geoff didn't play, but when he came home he was still full of excitement about it.

'It was a marvellous time, because in a way all the United players, first teamers and reserves, were all one unit. They liked a good time, but they didn't over-do things. All the players put their football first. But they loved cowboy films. If there was one on at the cinema they would all be there in the afternoon, just like big kids.

'Geoff liked modern music, Elvis and rock 'n' roll, and Shirley Bassey was one of his favourites. He also liked playing golf and tennis, and watching cricket. And we had a car, a Standard 10, in which we would often go out.

'Geoff was not moody or miserable but a happy type of man who could play jokes and take them when they were played back on him. I remember telling him I thought Mr Curry, the United trainer, looked a bit like Jimmy Durante, the comedian. Geoff told him this and the next time I saw Mr Curry he said "Oh, so you think I'm like Jimmy Durante, do you?" I was so embarrassed I didn't know where to put myself.

'He was a nice man, Mr Curry. So was Mr Whalley. Whenever I saw him he would always smile and say "Hello, Mrs Woman".'

There were often funny incidents. 'One day Roger Byrne had an accident driving to the ground. He was unhurt, but the car went off the road, smashed a wall and ended up in a garden, right under the front window of a house. The funny part was that of all the houses in Manchester, the car ended up at Matt Busby's next door neighbour's!

'Another time Freddie Goodwin's boots were stolen. They were so big, about size 13, that you couldn't imagine who would want them. When he heard about it, Geoff said: "Oh, yes, Freddie, I saw a couple of barges floating down the canal".

'Freddie had a little box car which he had to squeeze into. But he would sometimes give other lads a lift to the ground in it, though I still can't imagine how they managed to fit into it too. The ground was thick with snow one day and some of the lads decided to bury Freddie's car. They had nearly managed too, when Freddie arrived. He didn't think it was very funny, and he didn't give lifts for a while afterwards.

'When the team went to Wembley in 1957, some of the lads played cards on the train. Geoff was studying his hand when Wilf McGuinness just happened to be walking down the gangway. Wilf stopped, looked over Geoff's shoulder, and started announcing what cards were there. Geoff looked as if he could have murdered him!'

Marion thought for a moment and then said: 'George Best has come in for a lot of criticism, but I've always felt that what he needed to settle him down was a nice kind of girl. The trouble is, the girl he needs would be hard to find because of the life he leads.

'I remember when we used to go out, players, wives and girlfriends, there would always be some girls hanging around. They would be good looking and perhaps their clothes would be more expensive than ours, but they were not really interested in players as people, just as a way to get themselves into the spotlight. It used to amaze me how often these girls would manage somehow to get into the picture when we'd be out and someone would take a photograph.

'I once asked Tommy Taylor when he was going to settle

down and he gave me a smile and a wink and said: "When I get a girl like you who writes to her husband when he's away with the team". I think Tommy used to envy the lads who were happily married. A lot of the girls who used to hang around would have dropped him if he had stopped playing football.

'But Tommy did find a very nice girl, Carol. She used to come round to see me after Karen was born. So did Duncan's girl Molly, Mark's wife June, and Roger's wife Joy.

'When the boys would be playing away the wives would stay with each other, so that no one was ever left on her own.'

Geoffrey played twelve First Division games for United, two in the season of 1954–5, four in 1955–6 and six in 1956–7. One of his proudest moments came when he played against Tom Finney and a newspaper carried a picture of him taking the ball off the Preston and England star.

'Geoff could have commanded a first team place at any other club,' said Marion, 'but being understudy to a player as good as Roger Byrne held him back.

'He asked for a transfer but United wouldn't let him go. Several clubs wanted Geoff, including Wolves, but Matt Busby used to tell him, "There are no first team players here. You are all first team probables." And that was the way it was.

'He once put eight internationals into the reserves but they took it well and joked with the first teamers: "Oh, so you are not in the *real* team this week!"

'If you played badly, you were dropped. It was a case of two pounds for a win, one pound for a draw and a good telling off when you lost! But Geoff always knew that if Roger was fit, Roger would play. If Roger had been thirty-odd and towards the end of his career, it might have been different. But Roger was just reaching his peak. Geoff had gone as far as he could go with United.

'He got on well with Matt Busby, and I know the boss liked Geoff. But I would have liked Geoff to have had the chance to have succeeded or failed.'

Marion thought Geoffrey would have gone into business at the end of his career, probably as a joiner.

'Even when he was a full-time professional, Geoff still did some joinery in the summer. He liked the job, and when he wasn't making something for someone else, he would make things like a coffee table for the house. He made Karen's cot.

'He was a willing sort of person and became everybody's handyman, especially as he was at home during the afternoons. He would do all kinds of odd jobs for people. Three elderly sisters lived close to us and he would do a few jobs for them. When I came out of hospital with Karen, the sisters gave me clothes for her to show their appreciation for what Geoff had done for them. I think Geoff would have made a good businessman because although he was helpful, he was also fairly shrewd.'

As soon as possible after Munich, Matt Busby went to see Marion.

'I felt very sorry for him because he was so upset,' she said. 'He said he blamed himself for what had happened, for not stopping the third attempt at a take-off, but he said he hadn't interfered because others knew how to fly planes better than he did.

'My reaction to the whole thing came later. Because Karen was so young I was kept pretty busy, but as soon as she was three years old and starting to do things for herself a little more, I broke down.

'Karen is an only child but has never really felt like one because she has never been alone. She and my sister Betty's children were of a similar age and they all played together. Paul is two years older than Karen and Jackie a year younger.

'Paul plays football locally. He went to United for a trial and trained at the Cliff. I think he was a bit nervous. Anyway, nothing came of it.'

Karen is a pretty girl, very much like her father in looks and ways. 'Apart from anything else,' said Marion, 'Karen has

Geoff's complexion, nice and clear with not a freckle in sight. Not like me – I'm covered in them!'

After a brief interest in horse-riding, Karen, like her mother, began to go dancing. Her boy-friend, Mark Gill-banks, is a student at the Royal Northern College of Music (trumpet and piano) and lead trumpet in a local group, Vic Lezal's Professionals.

Mark's father, Harold, once played for United's 'A' team and reserve team. 'Apparently, he scored a goal for the reserves from a pass from Duncan Edwards,' said Mark.

Karen, who left school at sixteen to become a hairdresser, remembered her first visit to London as an eleven-year-old. She went to the European Cup Final with the Manchester United party.

'We took a taxi trip round for a quick look at the sights before the match,' she said, 'and then we got lost on the way to the Charing Cross Hotel, everyone was ready to go to the banquet.

'It was a really enjoyable trip, particularly the train journey home with the Cup, with so many people lining the track, cheering and waving long before we were near Manchester.'

Marion agreed: 'We got very excited at the match. Karen kept jumping in the air every time United scored, and an old chap kissed and hugged everyone when the ball went into the net.

'We appreciated United's gesture. It was very good of them. But I'd been to Wembley before, with Geoff and the lads we knew. I wished the players luck in 1968, but it's just not the same atmosphere if you haven't got someone of your own with the club.

'You have to be a mother or a wife of one of the lads to really feel a part of it.'

6. Roger Byrne

'Roger Byrne was morally one of the biggest men I ever met both as a captain and as a person. He was a wonderful captain with the moral fibre to fight the Club's battle with the players and the players' battle with the Club. Roger was very much a man.'
HARRY GREGG

The sun that had lured the tourists to Tunisia had disappeared and day had become dark evening as an excited group, alive with anticipation, made its way to a Turkish coffee bar. There, they were greeted by waiters and mingled with locals whose English was limited to 'Bobby Charlton', which they said with suitable reverence.

On this occasion, 29 May 1968, 'Bobby Charlton' was enough to get by with, and the guests sat on the floor with the others, attention focused on a television set specially installed for the European Cup Final between Manchester United and Benfica at far-away Wembley.

The locals joined the Britons in putting their voices behind United and everyone was hoarse after two hours of intense, emotional football, before Charlton and Matt Busby were seen to embrace with tears of triumph after a 4–1 victory in extra time.

When the television set was switched off, a boy of nine left the coffee bar in Tunisia with his mother and they returned to their hotel. They would have been at Wembley as United's guests, but their holiday had been arranged in advance of the club's progress to the final.

Still, the boy had watched from a distance as United

completed the job his father, as captain, had led them towards ten years earlier. Now it was time for bed at the end of a memorable day for Roger Byrne junior, the son a father knew nothing about. Not even the fact that his wife, Joy, had conceived a child.

'I had a forty-week pregnancy, and Roger was born thirty-eight weeks after his father was killed,' said Joy, who has since remarried and become Mrs James Worth, the wife of a schoolmaster.

Like his son, Roger Byrne was an only child, born at Gorton, Manchester, in September 1929. His father, William Henry Byrne, a Lancashire County bowls player and a football fanatic whose knowledge of the game would have destroyed any quiz master, died in March 1974, aged eighty. Mother, Mrs Jessie Byrne, is now living at Derby.

She remembered Roger's early days at Abbey Hey Junior School, Gorton, where he played football in a team of six and seven-year-olds and she went along to encourage him.

'One Saturday morning, when Abbey Hey were playing against another junior team, there were only two spectators apart from the teachers. Myself and a man, the parent of one of the other boys,' she said. 'After a while he said, "See that little lad over there? He'll be a good footballer one day."

'"That's my son," I told him.'

At eleven, Roger passed an entrance examination to Burnage Grammar School and played for the school and Burnage Boys. He sang in the choir at St James' Church, Gorton, and was a star gymnast with the Boys' Brigade ('Always the boy at the top of the pyramid,' said his mother).

There was no eager rush into football for the boy with the studious eyes and cleft chin. In fact, it was the furthest thought from his mind when he left school at sixteen with a Higher School Certificate and went to work as an apprentice in the laboratory of a dye firm.

'He was a good boy,' said his mother. 'A level-headed type, but generous too. He was given a two pounds bonus after his first two weeks at work and he brought the money home and gave it to me.

'Roger was not a particularly brilliant footballer when he was younger, and he didn't seem to have any ambition to become a professional player. It never occurred to me that he would be and I never encouraged him in that direction. I was more concerned that he settled well at a job.'

He spent two years in the Royal Air Force, playing football for his unit team and displaying enough all-round sporting ability for the RAF to want him to sign on for a further period to train to become a physical education instructor.

'He didn't fancy that,' his mother recalled. 'And he just carried on playing amateur football for a local team.' He also played cricket for the West End Club, Denton, with a promising lad called Brian Statham, who went on to become one of England's greatest fast bowlers.

United heard about a talented outside left called Byrne who played football for fun on their doorstep, and offered him a trial. He developed at Old Trafford with the great players of the 1948 FA Cup-winning team and he became a left full back with greyhound pace, mischievous guile and arrogant bearing. In fact, the heir apparent to the club captaincy was almost sent home from America by Matt Busby after being sent off in Los Angeles during a tour match.

United were playing Atlas, abrasive champions of Mexico, and, through captain Johnny Carey, Busby sent word to his players to stay calm in spite of provocation. Roger defied the instruction and would have been severely disciplined but for an apology to Carey.

'Yes, I've heard that Roger was a rebel when he was younger,' said Joy, 'but when I knew him he had grown out of that stage. I know Matt Busby thought a lot of him. The fact that he made him captain illustrates that clearly. And I know Roger had a lot of respect for Matt Busby and Johnny Carey.'

Joy and Roger met in 1954, when they were both studying

physiotherapy at Salford Royal Hospital. Having made his League debut for United in the 1951–2 season and established himself, he was already preparing for the future.

'Roger was a very intelligent man,' said Joy. 'He could have done well in virtually any profession, and while he was well established as a footballer he was thinking ahead. He knew where he was going.

'A lot of boys couldn't imagine football ending for them at thirty, thirty-one or thirty-two, but Roger was planning for that time. He was not studying physiotherapy as a means to stay in football, but primarily so that he would be a physiotherapist.

'I'm not saying he would have left football completely, but eventually physiotherapy would have been his work and football his sideline. He would not have gone into football management. Perhaps he knew the pitfalls that go with managing a football club.

'When I met him he had just returned from the World Cup in Switzerland and was studying in the afternoons. He was a famous footballer, but to the rest of us on the physiotherapy course he was just another student.

'The patients appreciated who he was more than we did, especially the youngsters at Pendlebury Children's Hospital. They thought it was marvellous to see a footballer.'

Roger's influence on the blossoming young United team grew from his own flair and consistency as a player and his personality as a man. He played 246 League games for United and won 33 England caps.

He mixed well with the players without becoming too close to them. Often he was thought to be slightly aloof. 'He was a natural leader for them in every respect,' said Joy. 'They respected him and in a way looked upon him as a father-confessor. The boys would go to him with some of their problems, and not only football problems.

'Roger was quiet but certainly not introverted. I would not say he was the serious type, except when it was necessary. He had a good sense of humour. He could see the funny side of things, and never took offence.

'He loved all sports and had become a keen golfer. He holed in one at St Andrews, I remember. He also liked to read and had a wide range of books. Travel books, novels, all kinds of subjects. He liked music, too, classical as well as modern.

'The people he got on with best were extrovert types like himself and he was always happy to join in any of the student pranks. He liked discussions and could put forward a good argument.

'When I met him he had a dog called Sandy, a Heinz 57, all-varieties mongrel. Sandy stayed with my mother-in-law when we were married but always waited for Roger to go round. He pined to death shortly after Roger died.'

Joy and Roger were married in June 1957. 'Roger was not a footballer at home or in our circle of friends. And to me he was always more a physiotherapist than a footballer,' she said.

'We didn't talk a lot about football, but he used to say that Tom Finney was a better player than Stanley Matthews and the only time I ever saw Matthews annoyed was when he was playing against Roger.

'He certainly didn't like criticism of his team from anyone. If people started to find fault with United to him he would say "You can criticize me, but don't criticize my team". He could always take criticism of himself not of another individual player or the team as a whole.

'But he could take a joke. When we were married and went to our honeymoon hotel, half the team turned up. And when we returned from honeymoon the house was a mess, covered in red and white streamers. But he just laughed it off.'

The FA Cup Final defeat by Aston Villa in 1957, when Villa winger Peter McParland charged and injured United goal-keeper Ray Wood, was a test of character for any player and particularly the captain. How did Roger react?

'He took it very well indeed,' said Joy. 'I know he was

bitterly disappointed but he did not show any bitterness. I think women show more emotion than the men, and the girls certainly showed their feelings more than the men after that Cup Final. We were very bitter about McParland.

'A month after the final Roger and I were married and went to Jersey for our honeymoon. While we were there, I came down from our room and saw Roger in the hotel bar, talking to some man as if he was his long-lost brother. The man turned out to be Peter McParland.

'I suppose that incident was a fair summary of sportsmanship, but I just couldn't swallow it. But I suppose women tend to bear grudges more than men.'

Roger was not an impatient type, but once behind the steering wheel of a car he liked to reach his destination as fast as possible. His driving was not without its problems. The crash into Matt Busby's neighbour's garden, for instance.

'Yes,' said Joy. 'He had to swerve that time to avoid a van coming down Wilbraham Road. But another time the car hit some ice and skidded into a lamp post.

'I knew Roger for three Februarys. The first February, he hit the lamp post. The second February, he swerved into Matt's neighbour's garden. And the third February, the plane crashed at Munich.'

Before United left to play Red Star Belgrade, there was concern over an injury to one of Roger's ankles.

Said Joy: 'There was a lot of speculation about whether or not Roger would go, but he would have gone even if his leg had been in plaster. He would have wanted to have seen the game. It was his team. His life.

'Ted Dalton, the United physiotherapist, treated the ankle and Roger played in the end. In fact he only missed one match in the time I knew him and that was because of a boil on his neck.

'He used to get injuries, of course. Cuts, bruises, strains, teeth knocked out, stitches in his eyes. All sorts of things. But he would manage to carry on.'

Joy continued her work as a physiotherapist. Roger died before he had qualified, though he had taken an intermediate examination.

'We were married for six months, but we did not see each other very often during that time,' said Joy.

'We were on honeymoon for two weeks and the day after we got back Roger had to have an operation on his nose, and that took two weeks. Then he was training, playing and studying.

'There were League games, European Cup games and other cup games. If he had a Monday off he would go to Salford Royal to study. Other days he would go there in the afternoon and he would spend weekends with the club, playing Saturdays and calling in at Old Trafford on Sundays.'

At twenty-eight, Roger had just about fulfilled himself as a football player, having travelled extensively representing both his club and country and having achieved as a captain all except the crowning glory of triumph in the FA Cup and European Cup.

'I wouldn't say he was looking forward to the day when his playing career came to an end,' said Joy, 'but he was more prepared for it than most players were. I don't think he would have regretted the day he would have had to stop playing as much as most of the boys would have.

'As for myself, I felt the sooner he came out of football the better. I suppose it depends on your sense of values. Football was a sport and entertainment, becoming more of an entertainment than a sport in fact. I just felt that Roger had more to offer.

'I think he had given a lot to football and had a lot to give to the medical world, and the world outside of football.'

Joy and James Worth and Roger junior are now living at Northenden, Manchester. Said Joy: 'United have always been very good to Roger and me. Very good indeed.

'Matt Busby is not the type of man to push his help at

people, but you always know he is there if you need his help. And if you do need it he will move mountains for you.

'Walter Winterbottom, the England manager when Roger was playing, has always been very keen to see young Roger. He will always make a point of getting in touch if he is in the area.'

Had Joy, very much an active, modern mother, any particular ambitions left?

'Just to be happy.'

Roger junior said he had often heard anecdotes about his father when people heard his name and asked if he was the son of *the* Roger Byrne. His father's caps and medals are carefully preserved in plastic covers.

'The impression I have of my father from all I have been told is of a very good footballer, a very good leader and a fine man,' he said.

Said Joy: 'Roger's father always wanted a son, and though he is probably like me in his looks he has his father's hair-colouring and his father's ways. He is very much like his father in temperament and abilities.'

It had been a busy day for Roger when I spoke to him. He had been cutting the back lawn after taking his first 'O-level' General Certificate of Education examination, maths, that morning. And he would be playing in a cricket match in the evening.

He said maths was one of his fairly strong subjects but it had been 'quite a difficult paper'.

Said Joy: 'I think today he's been more worried about tonight's cricket match than he was about the examination.'

The maths examination had been taken a year early. Next year he would have English, French, Spanish, chemistry, geography, history and physics to look forward to.

He hoped to go on to University when the time came to leave Manchester's famous William Hulme's Grammar School and his initial thoughts about a future career included forestry, a school games master and 'outdoor things like that. I wouldn't like to be trapped in an office. I just want to make enough money to be comfortable.'

His sporting activities included canoeing, cricket, rugby, skiing, swimming and tennis. Often he would go fell-climbing and his room was filled with books that betrayed another dream, to become a mountaineer.

'The man I most admire is Chris Bonington,' said Roger, 'and I hope soon to do some rock climbing.'

At William Hulme's, Roger plays rugby. Soccer is not part of the school's sporting life, though he did play centre half for Caius House, a private junior school at Urmston. 'I would describe myself as a dogged sort of player. I just keep going,' he said. 'If I am pressed about it, I suppose I prefer playing rugby.'

But, for three years from the age of nine, Roger was able to study First Division soccer from close range as a ball-boy at Manchester United. 'I started just before McGuinness was put in charge of the team and was still there when O'Farrell came,' he said.

'The atmosphere was fantastic, and, as ball-boys, you really get caught up in the games and are willing United to win. Sometimes you are tempted to throw the ball quickly for your own team and slow things down a bit when the opposition wins a throw or corner kick.

'But you can come in for quite a bit of abuse from visiting supporters. I've often had pork pies thrown at me, and when United played A.C. Milan in the European Cup, and their goalkeeper was injured by a missile from the Stretford End, I was on duty near the Cantilever stand. A lot of Italian supporters were there, and they threw all kinds of rubbish at me. It was all right at the Stretford End, in front of your own supporters.'

As a ball-boy, Roger saw a lot of his favourite player, George Best. 'He was brilliant,' said Roger. 'It was marvellous the way he would take on defenders twice his size and beat them with ease. There were so many sides to his skill. But he also had an Irish temper.

'I think it's fair to say that people my age tend to understand George Best a little more than older people and I think he's had to put up with quite a lot. The publicity, for instance, and all the people who wanted to know him just because he was famous.

'My view is that perhaps part of his trouble was that he earned too much money outside football. More than he did for actually playing. This gave him a certain independence, not relying solely on the club for his income.

'I don't think he loved football enough and I don't think his mind was completely on football. But you've got to hand it to him. He was brilliant.'

School rugby matches crowded in on Roger and he had to give up his job as a ball-boy, though he still watches United whenever he can.

'It's surprising how many of the boys I know switched from United to Manchester City when United started losing matches,' he said. 'But I've got a stand ticket, and I'll be at Old Trafford again next season. United need the support to be able to prosper.'

7. Eddie Colman

'Eddie Colman was one of those people you cannot say enough about. Wherever he was there was fun. I have never met before or since anyone with a bigger personality. It shone out of him. Eddie was one of the most underrated players, but he was a creator, an artist, and would have been one of the game's greats without the shadow of a doubt.'
WILF MCGUINNESS

The tricky little inside left suddenly became the star of Old Trafford, dazzling the opposition with three goals in seven minutes to put Ordsall Centre on their way to a 5–2 victory over Eccles Centre in the Salford Unemployed Cup Final. It was 1933, when hungry, out-of-work men were encouraged to play organized football to divert their minds momentarily away from their troubles and to keep them off the streets.

Dick Colman, unemployed for a total of five years, won a pair of heavy, working boots when his team became champions and a new suit was his prize after scoring a hat-trick in the cup final. Times were hard, and Dick pawned the suit for one pound. But his skill with a football brought him the more lasting reward of a job with an engineering firm. He may have been only five feet six inches tall but he was noticed, and given the chance of work and of playing for the firm in the Eccles and District League.

Dick, who was sixty-five in July 1974, a plate layer with the Manchester Ship Canal Company, recalled: 'Yes, I got a job through playing football, one of the lucky ones out of a crowd of men standing waiting for work.

'There were about a million other young men like us, but I was picked out and taken on by Gresham and Craven Engineering at Ordsall Lane. The firm's gone now.'

Dick continued to play amateur football for the Ship Canal team and Ashfield Labour Club, though the appearance at Old Trafford was the highlight of his career.

Three years after that final, his wife, Liz, presented him with a son. It was a difficult delivery, and Edward was the Colmans' only child, a youngster enriched with humour, generosity and a brilliant talent.

Edward, or Eddie as he came to be known to an admiring generation of football followers, was brought up in a two-up-two-down house in cobbled Archie Street, Salford – the original 'Coronation Street' of television fame. He lived at number nine, which was later to become the fictional 'Coronation Street' home of Elsie Tanner, buxom heroine of the durable soap opera.

Archie Street had a corner shop called Loates', an off-licence and general store, where locals would call with their jugs for three gills of ale. There was a church, St Clement's, but no 'Rover's Return'. No pub at all, in fact.

Just around the corner, in Wyatt Street, lived Eddie's cousin, Albert Valentine, who was six years older. Albert was evacuated during the war, but became Eddie's best friend.

'My mother, Evelyn, and Eddie's father were brother and sister and, like the Colmans, I had red hair,' said Albert, a progress clerk with an engineering firm at Trafford Park.

'Eddie's hair was fair to dark and I used to pull his leg by saying, "You're not a Colman because you haven't got red hair". That was something Eddie always longed for as a kid, red hair.'

Albert, an inside forward and, like Dick and Eddie, about five feet six inches tall, played a great deal of local amateur football and was good enough to have played alongside Frank Blunstone in the Crewe 'A' team.

'When I played for Ordsall Council School, Eddie would

be about six. He would carry my boots for me and I'd sit him on a blanket behind one of the goals,' said Albert.

'Eddie was always very quiet at home. That was the boy his mother and father knew. But outside he was a rum lad, and as a kid he was a villain, a genuine villain, always up to all sorts of tricks.'

Like Albert, he attended the local Ordsall Council School. 'He was no mug at school, but his reports always said that he was a better footballer than he was a scholar,' recalled Albert. 'His mind was always on football, and in the end it was football that made him.'

Said Dick: 'Eddie was always up to something and one day he came home from school looking pretty miserable and when I asked him what was wrong he said the sports master had left him out of the football team.

'I asked why he had been left out and he said "I don't know". It seemed odd to me, so I went to Ordsall School and saw Eddie's head-teacher, Miss Howard, about it.

'Miss Howard said she had asked the sports master to leave Eddie out of the team. "Why, was Eddie giving you cheek?" I asked.

'"No, not cheek exactly," she said. "He just gave me a look fit to poison me."

'I suppose that's what you'd call dumb insolence. Anyway, Eddie was punished by being left out of the team. Later, when he had made the grade, Eddie used to go to visit Miss Howard. He thought a lot of her.'

Eddie's mischievous ways did not cost him too many appearances in the school team, for he went on to play for Salford Boys and Lancashire Boys. He also played cricket for Salford and Lancashire Boys. 'Eddie was first wicket down,' said Albert. 'And Steve Fleet, the Manchester City goal-keeper, was in the same cricket team. Like Eddie, I played cricket for the school, and we both won cricket bats in a newspaper competition for the fastest centuries.

'As a footballer, Eddie started off as an inside forward, and was a good one. But another local lad, an inside forward, was an England Boys trialist, and Eddie was moved back to wing half. England Boys overlooked Eddie. I think they felt he was too small. A lot of lads seemed to suffer because of their lack of height.'

Eddie, the lovable rogue, was not an aggressive child and did not get involved in fights at school. But his impish ways sometimes brought him pain.

'When he was only about four, Dick and I were pushing a ball about in the house and he made a dive for it and caught his mouth on the corner of the sideboard,' said Albert. 'He got a fairly bad cut and had to have stitches in his lip.

'The scar was always there, in fact whenever Eddie laughed it seemed as if there were still stitches in his lip.'

Another injury was to play a vital part in his progress to football greatness.

Said Dick: 'Eddie hurt his back while playing in an air-raid shelter. He grew out of it, but the injury gave him a lot of trouble at the time. He was playing for Salford Boys and went to Old Trafford to have treatment for his back.

'United liked Eddie and Eddie liked them. Wolves would have liked him, but at the time it seemed certain that Eddie would be joining Bolton. But once he went to Old Trafford for treatment and saw what it was like, United became the club he fancied.'

Albert said: 'Yes, Eddie liked the set-up at United, and he was always a lad who made his own decisions. He would say, "If I'm going to fall by the wayside and become a docker, I'll do it on my own".

'He was a villain until he was about fifteen and then he turned out to be a gentleman – though I thought he would have been to Borstal before that happened!

'I think his good manners helped him at Old Trafford. He would always refer to the players as Mr Rowley and Mr Pearson and so on. He thought the world of Jack Rowley and though Rowley was always noted mostly for his shooting,

Eddie said he could centre a ball better than anyone he knew.'

When Eddie joined United, he gave his ten pounds signing-on fee to his grandfather, Dick Colman, a jolly man who died aged eighty-seven. If Eddie inherited his football skill from his father, his humour came from grandfather.

'Grandfather was a real comic,' said Albert. 'He used to tell jokes then that professional comedians are still telling today. Bobby Charlton and Wilf McGuinness would often be round at the house with Eddie, and they would gather round grandad and ask him to tell them some jokes.

'Eddie was always a joker, too. You'd never know what he'd do next. He'd put itching powder in your bed and all sorts of things like that. He was also very witty, but could be serious when he wanted to be.'

It was not long before Eddie's ball control and body-swerving elegance at right half earned him the name 'Snake Hips' at Old Trafford (scout Joe Armstrong once said: "Put a grass skirt on him and you've got a hula-hula dancer"), but his mother, who died in 1971, aged sixty-two, preferred not to watch him play.

'She was frightened in case Eddie made a mistake,' said Albert. 'I remember her going to a game against West Brom. United won easily, but Eddie's mother was frightened every time he got the ball in case he lost it. She just couldn't look.

'It's funny, because Eddie had all the confidence in the world. Nothing seemed to worry him. He just went out and played and even when there was so much competition for places at United he would just say, "Well, I'll go out and play and if there's someone who can play better then he deserves to be in".'

Eddie spent his National Service in the Royal Corps of Signals at Catterick, where, among other duties, he was the camp rat catcher. But during this time he continued to play for United.

He made the first of eighty-five First Division appearances

at Bolton in 1955, but even when he became an established star, his lack of height and boyish looks made it hard for some people to accept that he was one of the great United players. Commissionaires at football grounds, for instance.

'I remember a night match at Blackpool,' said Albert, 'when Eddie met me outside the ground with a ticket. We stood chatting for quite some time and when Eddie went to get changed the man on the gate wouldn't let him in and told him to go to the two-bob entrance for kids. He had to get Matt Busby before he was allowed in. And something similar happened at West Brom.'

Once out on the field, there was never any doubt that Eddie belonged to that United team.

'You can't teach a boy how to be a good footballer. Either he's got it or he hasn't,' said Albert. 'Eddie was always a good player, even with a tennis ball as a kid.

'I could see he had natural ability from the time he was about ten, and when he was fourteen or so, we played together against a dockers' team for a dollar a man on the park. I had some strong points in my game, but I didn't have the kind of ability Eddie had and I didn't have his guts. I moaned and groaned.

'He was great in possession and especially when coming forward. The ball was played to Eddie in midfield a lot. To my mind, the most important players in a team are numbers four and six, and eight and ten – the wing halves and inside forwards, and particularly the wing halves.

'I don't go in for the new names players have been given, like sweeper, because to me a sweeper is a man who cleans up with a brush. We've always had players covering the centre half. The wing halves are the key men because they carry most responsibility.

'If a team is not scoring goals, the wing halves are blamed for not putting the ball through accurately enough. If the team is conceding goals, the wing halves are blamed for not getting back to cover. The game revolves around their play.'

Not that Albert could not find flaws in cousin Eddie's play. Apart from being 'a bit weak in the tackle with his left leg' and 'heading a ball by jumping up, hunching his shoulders and hoping for the best', he treated the ball as if its case was made of mink rather than leather.

'Eddie was the same as his father. He couldn't hit a ball. That applied to playing cricket as well as football. Eddie and his father were both very good on the ball, but neither of them seemed to have the timing needed to give it a good whack. They would beat six players, be six yards from goal and have to pass the ball.

'Even when it came to passing, Eddie would push the ball accurately ten to fifteen yards rather than go for the long ball upfield.'

Dick Colman at least had that hat-trick at Old Trafford to look back on, which is more than could be said for his famous son.

'Eddie scored only two goals as a first-teamer,' said Albert. 'The first was at Tottenham, when United had half the first team out with injuries and drew 2–2.

'United were losing 2–0 at one stage and Eddie scored the equalizer. Duncan Edwards beat four men in a run down the left and put the ball across to Eddie on the six-yard line. Ted Ditchburn was in goal for Spurs and Eddie dummied him, sending him one way before pushing the ball into the other side of the goal.

'Eddie's other goal was scored against Red Star in the first match, at Old Trafford, when United won 2–1. The ball came across, and Eddie just slid it in.

'But Eddie's other abilities more than made up for any lack of shooting power. His control was brilliant. He could receive the ball on the touchline and beat an opponent by just body-swerving and rolling the ball back and forth with the sole of his boot. He could control a ball with either foot, too, and was excellent at moving into openings and creating space.

'He was also very fast. Roger Byrne was lightning over eighty yards, but the only player who could beat Eddie over a hundred yards was Ray Wood. Ray was the fastest man at Old Trafford.

'Eddie and Duncan Edwards were made for each other. Duncan was very shy and Eddie was anything but. They were different types, but they respected each other's play. And Duncan was a different person on the field to the one he was off the field.'

Eddie was an extrovert, except when it came to discussing football and personalities. Then, and when he was at home, he would be less than forthcoming with opinions.

'He was very well liked. In fact, he was a soft touch,' said Albert. 'He would give you his last halfpenny, even if he had never met you before.

'And he was very trusting, until someone gave him reason to be otherwise.

'Eddie always had time for people. He would listen to what they had to say, no matter who they were, even if he was stopped by a tramp, and he would thank them. He was very good-mannered.

'He wasn't the type that tried to make money out of selling tickets for the big matches. He just got the tickets for his family and friends. And he didn't talk about the game, except to me.

'After a match he would ask me "What did I do wrong?" and I would give my opinion and say, "Well, you were a bit weak here and a bit weak there". But eventually, when he made the grade, he didn't need to ask. Who was I to criticize then?

'Eddie would never criticize another player. Sometimes I used to say, "I don't fancy so-and-so" and Eddie would defend him by saying something like "But what would we do without him? He can hold things together."

'He admired Jack Rowley a lot and used to dream of playing on the same field as Matthews and Finney. Another of his idols was Ronnie Allen, of West Brom, but he was upset when they eventually met on a football pitch.

'Ronnie Allen fouled Eddie and Eddie went after him and floored him. That wasn't like Eddie at all. His idea of football was a game of skill and if he ever made a mug out of an opponent it was with sheer football.

'Eddie was too small to be a dirty player. It wasn't his game. But Bill Foulkes used to look after him if any of the big boys started getting a bit too rough.'

Football dominated Eddie's life but he loved to watch Salford Rugby League Club, the original 'Red Devils' ('How have Salford gone on?' was one way he had of deflecting questions about United) and he was a keen member of Salford Lads' Club, where he was known as a brilliant basketball player.

Like Albert, Eddie could relax by listening to records, but while Albert idolized Frank Sinatra and Nat King Cole, Eddie favoured the jazz of Kid Ory and Sidney Bechet.

Eddie had friends both inside and outside football. He was a natural mixer, though his closest friends from United were David Pegg and Tommy Taylor.

'David bought one of the first Vauxhall Victors when they came out,' said Albert, 'and the lads used to go off out together, to the Cromford Club or the Continental or a place called the Spare Wheel. Often, I'd go along with them.

'Eddie never smoked and three or four glasses of bitter or lager was his limit. He was religious in his work. He loved his profession so much that he would have played for nothing, never mind the seventeen pounds a week they got then.

'Every Friday night he would be in bed by nine o'clock. The only thing you could point to as any kind of lapse on Eddie's part was the fact that he was five minutes late for training every day. That became a club joke.

'Eddie used to walk from Salford every morning, and when he arrived Jimmy Murphy or someone would shout "Here he is, late again! Did they turn the bridge round to let the boat through again, Eddie?"

'He got on well with everyone, and there would always be someone up at the house. Mark Jones was a frequent visitor – a great lad. If you had committed a murder, Mark could convince you that you hadn't.

'Eddie was always pulling Duncan Edwards' leg, dancing with his girl, Molly, and cracking jokes. I used to say to Eddie, "You'd better watch out or one of these days Duncan will pick you up and throw you through a window".

'Eddie's girlfriend was a lovely girl called Marjorie, and they were close to becoming engaged. Marjorie is now married to Bobby English, one of the other United lads.'

Albert would have loved to be a football reporter. Eddie was just happy playing. He had no thoughts about a future career.

'And Eddie just loved flying. He would rather fly than travel in a car. In fact, if it had been possible, Eddie would have travelled from Salford to Manchester by air,' said Albert.

'When news of the crash first came, I kept in touch with Jimmy Murphy. At ten minutes past ten it was confirmed that Eddie was among those who had died. I told the family and then left the house. I just had to go out.

'I don't remember anything from that moment until I suddenly realized I was standing in Piccadilly, Manchester, after three in the morning, soaked to the skin without a coat and still wearing my slippers. The way I looked, I could have been arrested.

'After that, I didn't eat for two weeks, and I just could not settle to anything for two years. I couldn't sleep at night. I was shattered.

'Then, in 1960, an odd thing happened. I was lying in bed, unable to sleep as usual, when, in the early hours, I heard a car outside and people laughing. I then heard car doors slam, and the door of the house opened. Then there were footsteps on the stairs.

'I thought it must be burglars and got out of bed, grabbed a stick and waited. The bedroom door opened, and in walked

(*From the left*) Duncan Edwards, Eddie Colman, Mark Jones, Ken Morgans, Bobby Charlton, Dennis Viollet, Tommy Taylor, Bill Foulkes, Harry Gregg, Albert Scanlon and Roger Byrne line up before the match in Belgrade (*Popperfoto*).

BRITISH RAILWAYS

Youth International Match
ENGLAND v GERMANY
Wednesday, 12 March
Kick-off 7.30 pm

Next Home Match
1st DIVISION
United v
NOTTS. FOREST
28 Feb, Kick-off 3.0 pm

Team changes will be indicated by loudspeaker

MANCHESTER UNITED

Shirts Red — Knickers White

| R | FINNEY 11 | FROGGATT 10 | SHINER 9 | QUIXALL 8 | WILKINSON 7 | L |

O'DONNELL 6   SWAN 5   KAY 4

JOHNSON 3   MARTIN 2

RYALLS

FOOTBALL **GREEN** PLEASE

Referee: A. Bond, London
Kick-off 7.30 pm

Linesmen:
F. Wain, Bakewell — Red Flag
P. P. Clarke, Coventry — Yellow Flag

SHEFFIELD WEDNESDAY

Shirts Blue and White Stripes — Knickers Black

L   7   8   4   2   5   9   6   3   10   11   R

Thirteen days after the disaster, the United line-up for an FA Cup fifth-round fixture against Sheffield Wednesday was uncertain virtually up to the kick-off.

Matt Busby returns home (*right*) and takes his seat in the directors' box for the first time since the crash (*below, both Express Newspapers*).

(*Above*) Fifteen-year-old Duncan Edwards signs for Matt Busby; (*below*) Tommy Taylor, who started his career at Barnsley after being spotted playing for a local pit side.

(*Above*) David Pegg helps with the washing up (*Express Newspapers*);
(*below, left*) Mark Jones with his son Gary (*Express Newspapers*);
(*below, right*) Geoffrey Bent, a classy understudy to Roger Byrne.

(*Above*) Tommy Taylor demonstrates his prowess with the saxophone – Liam Whelan, Wilf McGuinness, Bobby Charlton and David Pegg are impressed. (*Below*) Tea at Mrs Watson's. Duncan Edwards passes Tommy Taylor the sugar, Mark Jones (next to Jackie Blanchflower) looks on, Bobby Charlton and Liam Whelan sit in front of the grandfather clock (*both Express Newspapers*).

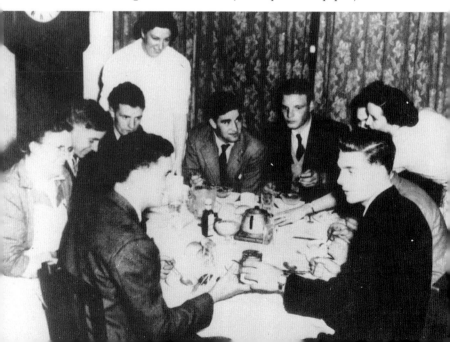

(*Above*) Matt Busby and Roger Byrne, right, toast League Championship success with the rest of the team. From the left: Johnny Berry, Bill Foulkes, Liam Whelan, David Pegg and Bobby Charlton. Eddie Colman and Tommy Taylor are standing. (*Below*) Matt Busby leads out the Cup Final side, May 1957 (*both Express Newspapers*).

(*Above*) The Busby Babes before one of their last European ties prior to the Munich air crash. Back row (from the left): Johnny Berry, Dennis Viollet, Ray Wood, Roger Byrne, Bill Foulkes, Duncan Edwards. Front row: David Pegg, Liam Whelan, Tommy Taylor, Jackie Blanchflower, Eddie Colman (*Popperfoto*). (*Below*) Training in the mud at the Yugoslav Red Army Stadium, 4 February 1958 (*Popperfoto*).

Eddie and David Pegg and said, "We're going to the Spare Wheel, are you coming?" I said "No" and they went and I heard the sound of a car being driven away again. I got back into bed and went to sleep.

'Next morning when I awoke I was sweating. I could not understand what I had seen, but I saw those boys perfectly clearly. I have no explanation for what happened. None at all. I only know that after two years of sleepless nights, I have had no trouble sleeping since that night.

'Eddie's memory will always be with me, but not in the same nightmarish way it was for those two years after the crash. And United have been fabulous to us. They could not have done more.'

Others have not been so kind to the memory of Eddie Colman. An Italian marble statuette of the player at his graveside at Weaste Cemetery was damaged by vandals. The statuette, with both arms missing and the head moulded back into place, now stands in the home of Dick Colman, for safe keeping, along with Eddie's football jerseys, trophies and pictures from the glory days.

There is a memorial plaque at Salford Lads' Club, and though Archie Street-cum-Coronation Street has gone for ever to be replaced by a new housing estate, there are two special high-rise blocks of flats in the Salford area.

One is called Eddie Colman Court, the other Duncan Edwards Court. Those boys celebrated twenty-first birthdays one month apart in 1957, Duncan in the October, Eddie in the November.

They would doubtless have shared much more but for the events of February 1958.

8. Duncan Edwards

'Duncan Edwards was a man in football but still a boy at heart. His ability was good enough for England but his potential was good enough for Heaven.'
JACKIE BLANCHFLOWER

A group of small boys once played a game in the yard of Wolverhampton Street Secondary Modern School, Dudley, Worcestershire. Each wrote his signature on a piece of exercise-book paper, and the strapping twelve-year-old they called 'Dunc' showed his paper to the others and said: 'You ought to keep that. One day that name will be famous.' They never did. It was just crumpled up and tossed away with the rest, because it was only a game.

Four years later, Duncan Edwards, aged 16 years and 184 days, played for Manchester United against Cardiff City in the First Division. Two years after that, aged 18 and 183 days, he became the youngest ever full England International player, winning the first of eighteen caps in April 1955 against Scotland at Wembley.

Miss Cooke, the arts and folk teacher at Wolverhampton Street, remembered Duncan as a star pupil, a boy of some nine stone, enormous for his age, but so light on those feet, with bells at the ankles; so beautifully balanced, so dainty.

The supporters of Manchester United, even those who stood on tip-toes at the furthest points of the stadium with necks craning, recalled the glorious blur of red and white as their team ran out of the tunnel and on to the field and the awesome size of Duncan's thighs. They knew him as the most formidable footballer of them all.

'He was always a big boy,' said his mother, Sarah Ann, a small, friendly woman. 'He was nine-and-a-half pounds at birth and put on two pounds every week.

'When I took him to the welfare clinic they would say what a lovely bonny baby he was. "We won't have to weigh him," they'd say. I gave him Ostermilk and can recommend it to anyone. Ostermilk and rusks.

'We didn't have the little tins of strained baby food then, but I wouldn't have used them anyway,' she added. 'I think they're too much for a young baby.'

Duncan was not an only child, but his sister, Carol Anne, born ten years after him, died after fourteen weeks. They are buried together at Dudley's Queen's Cross cemetery, and their headstone was unveiled by Matt Busby.

A stained glass window at St Francis's Church, where Duncan's memorial service was held, was dedicated to him and depicts him in the colours of Manchester United on one side and England on the other.

At the new home of his parents, a neat little bungalow in a cul-de-sac at Lower Gornal, Dudley, photographs of Duncan smile down from several walls; the boy with fair hair and a face of mischief, the soldier of National Service days, the footballer, all muscle in a United jersey.

The lounge is dominated by a large wood and glass cabinet, the showcase of a son's achievements, with rows of international caps awarded at schoolboy (he captained England), youth and full England levels, two League Championship medals, Youth Cup medals and plaques, souvenirs of travel abroad, books, and a replica of the 'Duncan Edwards Cup', the commemorative trophy of a keenly contested local competition.

On top of the cabinet, among other framed memories, is a five-pound note in a special display case. 'It was the last Duncan gave to his mother,' explained his father, Gladstone

Edwards, adding, 'He gave a note to me at the same time, but I must have spent it.'

Not all the mementos are works of fine craftsmanship. There is Duncan's fishing tackle, his old cricket bat and some small, solid rubber balls he used to kick around as a toddler.

'Duncan could kick before he could walk. He would kick everything,' his mother said. 'And as soon as he could walk he was kicking more than ever. It didn't have to be a ball. A stone, a brick, anything.'

She formed her hands into half circles and joined them to show a diameter of about six inches and said: 'It was not long before I bought him a little case ball, about this size. And then I got him some little football boots, which were continually having to be replaced because of wear and tear or because his feet were getting bigger.

'His shoes! They were always in a mess from kicking a ball or a brick. He would spend hours just kicking a ball or heading it against a wall. He would head it and keep it going against a wall for ages. He never walked to school, which was about a mile from home. He kicked a ball all the way there and all the way back again.

'I never had to teach my boy to play football the way Bobby Charlton's mother did. He was just born with the ability. It was natural. He kicked a ball without anyone ever showing him how.'

His father is now retired and is troubled by a chest complaint. He spent the greater part of his working life polishing metal at a factory in nearby Bilston, but in 1964 he became a garden assistant at Queen's Cross cemetery and, latterly, had a similar job at Gornal Wood Crematorium.

During his days at Queen's Cross, truck drivers from Manchester would often make a short diversion to visit him and to see Duncan's grave, and the London members of the United Supporters' Club often made a pilgrimage to the graveside and visited Gladstone's home when the club was playing a match in the Midlands.

'I remember the times I used to tell Duncan as a little boy not to bring a ball with him when we went visiting. But no matter how often I said it, he always managed to hide a ball away somewhere.

'He liked to be carried. But once we arrived, out would come the ball and off he would go. There was no stopping him then.

'I remember walking down the street one day and seeing him playing football in the local park. An organized game, with a proper ball and boots. He was only ten and was playing with boys of sixteen and seventeen. I didn't know he was playing with the older boys until then. But he was managing all right. And he was as big as them, anyway.'

Said mother: 'Duncan was never any trouble to me and was always a healthy child. Oh, he had the odd cold and things like that, but they didn't keep him down for long. He'd soon be off out again to play with the big lads. They loved Duncan. I can hear them now saying, "Come on, Dunc, we're picking sides". They would pick sides and then argue which one would get Duncan.

'One day I heard them talking and one of the boys said, "What are you going to do when you leave school, Dunc?" And he answered, "I'm going to play for Manchester United". Even then, United was his team.'

A team-mate at Wolverhampton Street School was Ken Smith, who now runs a pub, the Cross Keys at Lower Gornal.

Often on Saturday nights Duncan's parents would visit Ken's pub for a quiet drink, and when he got to know them better, Ken produced a photograph of the Wolverhampton Street team of 1949, with Duncan, the captain, with the ball in his lap, and Ken, the right full back, standing in the back row.

'It was the under-fourteen team, and though we all had blue shirts and white shorts very few of us had the same style or colour of socks,' he said. 'They used to throw the boots and socks in a pile and tell us to go and sort out what would fit.

'In those days it was harder for schools to come by football kits, but we loved the games all the same.'

Ken and Duncan came from different districts of Dudley and went to different junior schools, finally teaming up at Wolverhampton Street.

'The estates were split by a ridge of limestone and fossils,' said Ken. 'Duncan went to the Priory Junior School and I went to Wren's Nest Junior School. When I met him at Wolverhampton Street we were in different years. I was a year older than Duncan and I would be in class 4a when he was in 3a. There were about thirty to a class.

'He was a quiet lad who kept himself to himself and mixed only with his own crowd.

'There were lads at school you could call bullies but no one ever bothered Duncan. He was always left alone. I can't remember anyone picking a fight with him.

'He was Miss Clarke's favourite. We used to do folk dancing and Duncan was great at it. He put as much style and balance into his dancing as he did into his football. He liked cricket, too, and was a pretty good batsman.

'When we were in the school football team he was always outstanding. He used to be in the forwards then and I know how good he was because when we played practice games I would come up against him at right back. And I had no chance, I can tell you! No chance!'

The team of 1949 did not bring Duncan instant fame and a trophy to hold aloft. 'We reached the final of the Dudley Schools' Under-fourteen Cup but lost 2–0 to Dudley Grammar at the local sports centre ground,' said Ken.

'I don't remember much about Duncan's school reports,' said his father, 'and if he had homework, I can't remember seeing it.'

His mother added: 'He must have been all right at school, though, because we never had any complaints. The teachers would always be round at the house for a chat. They all liked Duncan.

'He loved the open air. He was in the Scouts and loved to go camping. And animals! He had pigeons and rabbits and would have turned our place into a farmyard if we'd let him. He had a black and white collie dog, too, but I can't remember its name.'

'Jimmy,' said father.

'If there was a circus anywhere near he'd want to go to see the animals,' said his mother. 'He liked pantomime, too. And used to be good at sketching.

'He liked a joke and a bit of fun, but he was never a show-off. If he'd been playing with the England Schoolboys team he'd just come in, say "Hello, mum", put his bag down and go out to see the boys.

'If he'd won a trophy or a medal he wouldn't come into the house waving it in front of us or anything like that. He always left me to open his bag and find anything he might have won.

'We got a television set – twelve-inch model – when he started playing for the England Schoolboys. We loved to watch him play. I remember in one match he took the ball off five other players. Five of them!'

Was Duncan's skill in any way hereditary?

His mother thought: 'My father, Henry, played a lot of football in his local league. He died young. He was in his early thirties. And there was Duncan's father's brother, George. He used to play.'

Said father: 'Yes I played with George in a Cradley Heath league, but we never reached any great standard. George was the right back and I was at left back.'

Like Roger Byrne?

'I wish I could have played like him,' he smiled. 'No, I wasn't that good. I was about the same build as Duncan – six feet one inch and about thirteen-and-a-half stone. But as Duncan got older that's where the similarity ended, because he was always so fit from his football.

'That was my mistake, not keeping so fit. That's why I'm the way I am now.'

Duncan was fifteen when he left Wolverhampton Street School and signed for United. 'People around here were always disappointed that he did not go to one of the local clubs, Wolves, Birmingham, Villa or Albion,' said Ken Smith. 'My favourite team was always Wolves. I thought Jimmy Mullen was great. But Duncan always had this thing about United.

'But when he came to the Midlands playing for United people would go to the matches just to watch him. And when he played for England he was always "Our Dunc".'

Said his father: 'At one time I used to watch Albion, mainly because the lads I went about with supported Albion. But with Duncan it was always the same. United. Even though we were surrounded by Wolves, Birmingham, Albion and Villa and others like Coventry and Walsall.

'His favourite player was Stanley Matthews.'

'Yes,' added mother, 'and he was thrilled when he was able to play with Matthews for England. But he used to take the ball off Matthews as well!'

When United joined the queue of clubs competing for Duncan's signature, there was no contest.

'Not only was Duncan keen to go to United, but when Matt Busby came to see us I was impressed right away by his manner. And as soon as he started to talk, that was it,' said father.

'Yes,' agreed his mother. 'The first time we met Matt Busby it was obvious that he was a gentleman. But right from the time clubs started showing interest in him, I told Duncan that it was important to have another trade to go with his football because you could never tell how things would work out.

'He decided to take up cabinet making. I remember that when Bolton wanted to sign him and we went up to see them, they said they would help Duncan to learn the trade. And when he went to United, it was still cabinet making.

'When he first started with United he did take it up but as soon as he got into the first team, he dropped it. And he never told us what he'd done. We found out for ourselves.'

Duncan was not one to push his problems on to others.

His mother said: 'He never told me if he had any kind of troubles. He didn't want to worry me. If I heard anything at all, it would come from someone else.

'I think he must have been a bit homesick when he first went to Manchester. He used to bring me down his washing. And he always had a bunch of flowers for me.

'But after a while he stopped bringing down his washing and instead must have taken it to a laundry. It was a sign that he was settling up there.'

Then the army moved in. 'We saw less of him – in fact we never saw him in uniform,' said mother. 'He didn't like the idea of going into the army for National Service. He just wanted to play football. But that's what he did anyway. He played for the army and United and never got time for anything else.'

Said father: 'I used to go to Manchester every other week when Duncan was playing and the game that sticks out in my mind more than the others was the one against Bilbao at Maine Road. What a wonderfully exciting night that was, with United, down from the first leg of the tie, fighting back to win.

'I remember Di Stefano playing for Real Madrid. He was some player, that Di Stefano.'

'Duncan wouldn't do anything that might interfere with his football. That's why he would still have been playing today,' said mother. 'He liked to go to the pictures and the theatre. If there was a good show on he'd go as often as three times a week.

'Food was never a problem. He would eat anything as long as it was wholesome and properly cooked. He loved fish and chips, especially when he'd been to the pictures. He'd buy some on the way home and eat them out of the paper.'

There is a picture of Duncan with his fiancée, Molly, who has since married and lives in Somerset. There are also pictures of her two children.

Said Duncan's mother: 'Molly's a Manchester girl. She has kept in touch with us and still writes and visits.'

Mother turned the pages of a large photograph album and the years flashed back with every portrait or action shot of Duncan and the other Babes. 'You know, those players were made for each other,' she said. 'They all just moulded together.

'We used to go to a lot of the games together and all the mothers and wives and girlfriends mixed very well. A lot of the boys were in digs together in a house just off Warwick Road, up from the ground. Duncan was with lads like Tommy Taylor, Billy Whelan, David Pegg, Jackie Blanchflower and Bobby Charlton.

'It was lovely watching them play in those days. The football just flowed from them. That team would have beaten the world. We used to laugh at the way Duncan would leap up and down, warming up before the kick-off.'

Mr and Mrs Edwards have kept in touch with United. 'We are still invited when something special is on,' said mother. 'And you still couldn't keep us away from football when it's on the television.

'But though we watch it, we don't enjoy it as much as we used to. It's not the same today. Players seem to go for each other more than they go for the ball.'

Duncan was not eighteen when he came face to face and will to will with Jimmy Scoular, the tough, uncompromising captain of Newcastle United, in the centre circle at Old Trafford.

It was a 50–50 ball, and for what must have been the only time in his life, Scoular gave way to his youthful adversary. He would never admit whether he backed away from the confrontation out of discretion or diplomacy.

Jackie Milburn, the great Newcastle and England centre forward of the 1950s, remembered his first meeting with Duncan: 'This big lad came up to me at the start of the game and said, "Reputations mean nothing to me and if you come near me I'll kick you over the stand". And that's just what he tried to do as soon as I got the ball. United beat us 5–2 in that game. What a team they had – and what a player that big lad Duncan was. He was a nice lad too, for all his size and power. After the game he came to me and said, "It was a pleasure playing against you".'

Every career has a particular highlight and Duncan's had many. But perhaps the one best remembered, because of circumstances and environment, was the time he played against West Germany in Berlin in 1956.

The Germans were the World Cup holders from 1954 and the pride of that nation was bursting from every seam of the stadium. Squeezed in among them was a group of British soldiers determined to let the England boys know they were not without support.

Suddenly, Duncan put all his strength and dexterity into one of those famous runs that earned him the affectionate nickname 'Tank' from United supporters. The Germans who attempted to stop him were brushed aside. Nothing could stop Duncan from crashing in a goal that helped beat the Germans 3–1 and delighted the handful of Tommies.

Duncan's first class career from the day he made his First Division debut to the afternoon he sat in the Elizabethan at Munich airport, aged twenty-one, spanned only four years, nine months and six days, in which time he played 151 First Division games and one season played a total of 92 matches.

A glimpse of greatness. Yet Duncan was to football what Jack Nicklaus is to golf: all-powerful and dominating, a head and shoulders above worthy challengers.

Johnny Miller, emerging as a new young star of United States golf, said of 'Golden Bear' Nicklaus: 'When Jack's good, he finishes first. When he's bad, he's second. And when he's awful, he's third.'

Opponents used to feel that way about Duncan, for even when he had an off-day he still had the beating of them.

A road now runs where Wolverhampton Street School once stood and the boys played their games. But 'Dunc' was right. They ought to have kept his piece of paper.

9. Mark Jones

'Mark Jones was a very solid character. He was my ideal as a centre half, big, very strong and commanding in the air. He once told me he wished he could do things like me, "in cold blood". A nice fellow and a fine player.'
BILL FOULKES

Mark Jones had three ambitions. He wanted to play centre half for England, to take part in an FA Cup Final and to shake hands with the Duke of Edinburgh. He achieved none of those things, but came close to two of them.

An eye injury prevented him from playing for Manchester United against Aston Villa in the 1957 final, though the debate whether to risk Mark or select Jackie Blanchflower continued almost to the eve of Wembley. He did see his team-mates shake hands with the Duke, whom he greatly admired, but, as a reserve with Dennis Viollet, he could only look on from the trainers' bench.

It is fair to add that, at twenty-four, the ambition to play for England was within reach, and Mark did captain England Boys and play schoolboy international matches at centre half, left back, right half and left half during one season.

Gary Jones, aged eighteen, has but one ambition. He wants to see his team, the team he supports, Manchester United, play in an FA Cup Final, though he did once tell his mother, June: 'If I had been a footballer I would like to have done the three things my dad wanted to do.'

Gary is a Wombwell Branch 'Stretford Ender', with the uniform of a red and white bob-hat and scarf tied round the waist, and he defends himself against the stigma of that odious order of Old Trafford by stressing: 'It's just a minority of fifteen and sixteen-year-olds who drink under age, run on to the pitch, fight and cause damage, who give the rest of us a bad name.

'I travel with a couple of other lads from Wombwell and we go to watch the football. We like the atmosphere of the Stretford End. I missed only five home games last season and those were in midweek when it was hard to get there.'

June, Mark's widow, a red-head, owns up to past displays of temperament from her seat near the players' tunnel at Old Trafford, recalling: 'I used to hit people over the head with my handbag if they shouted names like "dirty Jones" when Mark committed a foul or if they threw other abuse at him when he made a mistake.'

But that was long ago. June, now remarried for eleven years to Herbert Barker, a friendly, understanding man who earns a living driving the lorry he owns, has not watched a match at Old Trafford since Munich and goes shopping when a Cup Final is on television.

'If I went to United now I wouldn't see the players of today,' she said. 'I'd see Mark and his pals passing the ball to each other and laughing together. I'd see Mark limbering up, jumping in the air and throwing his arms up.

'When the Cup Final is on I'm only interested in seeing the players and their wives on television when they're getting ready for the game. I know just how they are feeling.'

Gary was two years old when he lost his father. His sister, Lynn, was four months from being born. They were late in coming to know about their father's profession and the game he loved.

Said June: 'Gary never kicked a ball until he was seven, because I wouldn't give him one. I didn't even talk to him about football. I was too upset about Mark and frightened that the same might happen to Gary.

'But when he was seven, I went to see his headmaster, Mr

Wroe, who also used to teach Mark. I talked to Mr Wroe about something concerning Gary and he brought up the subject of football and asked if Gary had it in him like his father. I told him that if Gary wanted to play it was all right, but not to make him play just because his father played.'

Gary, centre half for his school, followed his father's example by playing in defence for Don-on-Dearne Boys, at right back, though his preference was right half.

Mark was six feet one-and-a-half inches and fourteen-and-a-half stone. His son is developing along similar lines, at six feet and thirteen-and-a-half stone. Not unnaturally, United took an interest in Gary and offered him a trial.

'I was due to go to train at United for about ten days during one Christmas. I broke my right leg playing for Don-on-Dearne at Doncaster and I'd only had the plaster off a few weeks when I went for my trial at United. I didn't impress anybody, and after that I gave up the idea of being a professional footballer,' he said.

'I still play in a few local games, but I have put on weight with the injury and a bit of drinking and, anyway, lads of my age are playing League football, not just starting.'

But he did follow his father in another way, by going into the building trade, and he was happy to take up bricklaying with a course at technical college.

Said June: 'Mark was a bricklayer. He always wanted a trade behind him in case things went wrong with football. And he loved to work outdoors. Gary's the same. He started off as a joiner but he didn't like that. He wanted to be working outside.

'Lynn is still at school. She was interested in veterinary surgery until she heard that would involve staying on at school. Then she thought she might get a job in printing, but that fell through. It looks now as if she'll probably get a job in a chemist's shop at Barnsley.

'When Gary started playing football, I didn't discourage him, but I didn't encourage him either. I left it up to him. It can be a good life for lads now and if he hadn't broken his leg he might have done something.

'But I'm not disappointed he didn't become a footballer, though it depressed him a bit when the leg injury handicapped his chances in the trial. He hasn't bothered about thinking of football as a career since, though he's crazy about United.

'It's not really because of Mark. United is just Gary's team. Though I haven't been to Old Trafford, I did take Gary to the European Cup Final. United invited us, and I went for Gary's sake. United have been very good to us all along. And Les Olive, the secretary, always sends Gary tickets for the games.'

Gary still has pictures of George Best on his bedroom wall, though he admitted he was not impressed with George's behaviour off the field.

'I idolized him,' said Gary. 'And I like Big Jim Holton. He's a good, honest sort of player. I've got a lot of time for Jim. I started watching United a few years back and sold my fishing rod so that I could afford to go to Bolton for the Cup semifinal replay against Leeds. I didn't think they'd go down last season and I lost a bit of money on it.

'We've still got some fair players, but we need to get a good start next season. I hope this new lad, Pearson, is going to score some goals.'

Said June: 'Gary won't have anything said against United. I've told him about the team they used to have, the one his father played for, the one that would have been the greatest ever. But he just can't take it in.

'He thinks today's team is great and thinks the fuss over the old team is just sentiment. He doesn't understand. When I talk about the team I knew he says I'm biased. Perhaps I am, because we all grew up together. The boys grew to be men. And it was a great team.

'Though Gary and Lynn are both like Mark in looks and ways, Gary and I do have a similar temperament. We both flare up easily. The difference is that Gary won't bear malice, but I will. I'll still be simmering and not speaking when, as far as he is concerned, the whole thing is over and done with.

'He's like Mark in another way. When I would lose my temper, Mark would hear me out and then say "Have you done?" And he would tell me, "Look, June, I can be led, but not driven". Gary is just the same.'

Mark was born at Low Valley, between Darfield and Wombwell, about four miles from Barnsley, and he attended Darfield Foulstone Modern School, where he played football, climbed trees, had a few fights and was, to quote June, 'a bit roguish'.

His father, Amos, a time-keeper at the old Wombwell Main colliery, fancied Mark would make a good class boxer and encouraged him to start punching his weight at the local youth club. But his mother, Lucy, was the real driving force behind Mark's progress in football.

'She used to be full of it,' said June. 'Not quite like Bobby Charlton's mother, teaching him to play, but full of encouragement. She used to watch Mark wherever he played. She even organized coach trips from Wombwell to go to matches.'

Lucy Jones died in November 1957 and June recalled: 'Her last words to Mark were "Oh, I'll worry about you and your football".'

Amos Jones died a few years ago, leaving two sons, Tom, who played football at Bradford, and Amos junior, whose sport was running. Both boys were born before Mark. There are also three sisters, Mary, Hilda and Irene, the youngest of the family.

Mark met June when he was fifteen and she a year older. 'I couldn't believe he was only fifteen,' she said. 'He looked more like twenty.' Their courtship lasted five years.

'He was a bricklayer when I met him,' said June, 'and I didn't know he played football. It was twelve months before he even mentioned it.'

Elsewhere Mark's football was well known. Barnsley were

keen to sign him, but he went straight to United to meet up with two of his idols, Allenby Chilton and Stan Pearson.

Johnny Steele, Barnsley's general manager and secretary, recalled: 'I was overseas in the forces when Barnsley tried to sign Mark and I only heard about it when I came back.

'He was big and a great header of a ball, but I used to think he was a wee bit crude. When I came back from the forces I had a bad knee, but I played in the reserves for a while and played against Mark a couple of times. At the time I wasn't particularly impressed.

'I think the great players around him then, like Aston and Carey, helped make him into the fine player he became. They were great players for a youngster to develop with. They gave him confidence and that came through in the great side United built.'

Mark was seventeen when United gave him the first of 127 First Division games. That start was against Sheffield Wednesday in October 1950.

'At first, Mark was in digs with a lot of the other boys, Jackie Blanchflower, Tommy Taylor, Duncan Edwards, David Pegg, Bobby Charlton and Gordon Clayton at Mrs Margaret Watson's house near Old Trafford,' said June.

'I used to see him at weekends and holidays and went over to Manchester for a lot of matches. We stayed at Mrs Watson's for three weeks when we were first married and we were waiting for our house. We moved into Jack Crompton's house in King's Road.'

June and Mark had been married four years in the January before his death at Munich on 6 February 1958, his mother's birthday.

'Mark was everything that is good, and I'm not just saying that because he's gone,' said June. 'They called him the gentle giant, and though he could dislike people he could never hate anyone. He would never have a bad word for teams who beat United or even players who kicked him.

'Gary was always his first thought when he got home, and

he loved his family and home. He was a home bird really. And a country man, not a city man.

'More often than not he wore a trilby and smoked a pipe and he liked to wear tweeds and go walking. One of his hobbies was shooting. He had a black labrador dog called Rick which he would take off to shoot at a farm in Cheshire. He used to say, "One day, when I retire, we'll live out in Cheshire". I still have his guns upstairs. I kept them for Gary.

'Mark liked to make things. He made a case for the guns. He also made an aviary for the budgerigars and canaries he bred.

'His brother Tom took Rick when Mark died, but the dog only lasted for about another twelve months. I think he pined a little. We gave away Mark's fifty-two birds. We put an advertisement in a Manchester paper about them and had a queue of children all down King's Road.

'I remember when Mark learned to drive and we got our first car, a lime-green Morris 1000. And he played a bit of golf. He was always out and about. He would go down to the ground, then off shooting. Sometimes he would take Gary along, though Gary can't remember anything about his father.

'But above everything else, Mark loved his football. He used to tell me he would play for nothing, and he would go to all the charity functions, knocking over piles of pennies and opening fêtes, things like that. He was the type of man who would carry an old lady's shopping basket. And I often used to see him helping the supporters in invalid carriages just before kick-off time on match days.'

Life in Manchester for June was that of the ordinary housewife, though occasionally there were celebrations and laughter. 'I sometimes think it's never happened,' said June. 'But I really enjoyed my four years in Manchester. All the players would come to our house from time to time. David Pegg lived with us for six months.

'Whatever was happening, United always made sure no

one ever felt left out. We were all made to feel important. I remember one time Matt Busby, now Sir Matt, of course, put his hand on my shoulder and said, "Always remember, June, behind every good man there's a good woman".

'That sort of thing always helped to let you know that United cared. The team used to be away a lot, what with tours and European games, and I remember one day I saw Tom Curry, that marvellous man who was trainer. In a joking sort of way I said, "What do those lads get up to when they're away?" and he looked me straight in the eye with that way he had and said, "June, I don't have to tell you. If they were all like your Mark, no one would have to worry."

'Mark was not a drinker. He would occasionally have a shandy, but was certainly not a beer man. In fact his main drink was pineapple juice.

'People would always pull his leg about the pineapple juice. We went to Jeff Whitefoot's birthday party and someone got a bottle of pineapple juice, emptied it and filled it with whisky.

'Mark didn't know and thought they were just joking as usual when they said "Come on, we bet you can't drink that bottle of pineapple in one go". Mark said "Of course I can", and did.

'He wasn't a drinker, as I've said, and that whisky put him out. We had to stay the night. We used to have some fun, though. Mark and Eddie Colman used to give a cabaret, singing "Frankie and Johnny".' Mark had a dread of flying. He would not say a great deal about it, but would always sigh with relief when the aircraft touched down and he was able to step back on the ground again.

'After the crash, Harry Gregg brought home Mark's belongings. He had his trilby, which he wanted to keep. Mark had bought a toy for Gary, a clown playing a drum.

'A lot of people wondered why I didn't have Mark buried in Manchester. Before Gary and Lynn came along we had a daughter who died at birth. She would have been twenty now. She was buried in Manchester. But Mark always used to say, "If anything ever happens to me I want to be buried back home in Wombwell".

'I went back home, too, though not because I was short of friends in Manchester. I just felt I could cope better at home, where I had relatives, and that it would be better for the children.

'The odd times I went back, when Gary was still very small, I would be ready to leave to come home again and he would be standing near the door. I would say "What's wrong?" and he would say, "I'm waiting for my daddy". It only seemed to affect him like that when we went to Manchester.

'I tried not to talk about Mark to the children for a long time. Then one day Gary came home from school and asked, "Why haven't I got a dad like the other boys and girls?" and that was it.

'Gary would be about three when Matt Busby asked to see us. He particularly wanted me to bring Gary. Mr Busby was recovering well but was still using sticks to get around.

'He had been seeing all the people close to the players who died. And when he saw me he put his head on my shoulder and cried. I've always thought it wonderful that such a big man could feel so deeply as he does. His wife, Jean, was very nice too.

'I remember before we left he patted Gary on the head and said, "Well, we've got a future United centre half here", and he was almost right about that. United have always been very good to us in many different ways. They have never forgotten us.'

Outside the neat semi-detached house, Herbert Barker was busy shovelling into his lorry the debris left after work on an extension to the kitchen.

'Herbert is a good man. He didn't know I was Mark's widow when we first met, but it didn't make any difference when he did. And he's very good to the children. He's had to put up with quite a lot, though. People saying how he landed on his feet and such like. But anything Herbert has he's worked for. And he's not the type to let talk bother him.

'We're well settled here. I don't regret moving back from Manchester. I have relatives and friends here. It's where I'm from. And, though I know it's not the sort of thing to say, Mark's grave is just around the corner and I can visit it every day if I want to.

'I sometimes feel that Gary resents not having known his father, without realizing he does resent it. That's the sad thing, that the children have been cheated out of knowing their father. I'm not talking about money or anything like that. Just knowing him.'

10. David Pegg

'David Pegg was the complete left winger, a brilliant ball player. Whichever of us was in the first team would be shunned by the other, but this was rivalry, not bitterness. David was one of the boys, always someone to be respected, and if he ever got there first, as he did with me, it was very difficult to shift him.'
ALBERT SCANLON

It was a wet and windy afternoon in the World Cup June of 1974, but for Sean David Beevers, aged eight, there was a special treat. Grandmother Pegg allowed him to wear uncle David's one and only senior England international cap. Sean had wondered about that cap and another for schoolboy international matches, plus the medals, plaques and other assorted trophies, one each year from 1950 to 1957, displayed in a cabinet in the lounge of his grandparents' bungalow at Scawthorpe, near Doncaster.

Now, for the first time, the cap, England versus Republic of Ireland 1957, was on his head and he was surprised what a good fit it was and how it felt. Looking at it through the glass of the cabinet, he had imagined it to be hard, like cardboard.

'Oh, Nana,' said Sean, 'it's soft and fluffy.'

Having satisfied his curiosity, Sean handed back the cap to grandmother, Mrs Jessie Pegg, and returned to a game of family bingo.

Sean got to know about uncle David's fame as a footballer the day his sister, Sara, aged ten, asked her mother, Mrs Irene Beevers: 'Why have I only one Christian name when Sean has two?'

Irene explained that Sean was also called David after his uncle, who had played for Manchester United. Irene was good at explaining to children. Her six years' experience as 'Auntie Irene' in charge of a local play group had helped her into a new job at Bentley Rehabilitation Unit.

'Sean is a lot like our David. Quiet and placid,' said grandmother. 'But Irene was like David, too. Sean likes to kick a ball, but I don't know whether he'll ever make a footballer. He likes drawing and pulling toy cars and aeroplanes to pieces and putting them together again.'

Grandmother Jessie and her husband Bill have another daughter, Doreen, married with two daughters, Jackie and Kim, and living in Australia. She was due to visit them at Christmas.

Doreen, born two years after brother David, was the one who once bloodied his nose.

'David used to tease the girls a lot, but they could stick up for themselves and used to pick at him when he came home when he was playing for United,' said mother.

'I remember the time Doreen and David were in another room. He must have gone a bit too far with his teasing, and she must have given him a good thump by the look of his nose when he came in. I thought "good for her".'

David was not the type to go looking for trouble. He was always too busy playing ball games, fishing or swimming. But he was not soft.

'He was never any bother and never brought us any trouble, but he did once have a fight with a neighbour's lad,' said mother. 'I don't know who started it or what it was all about, but the other lad was quite big and a few years older and he came off worse. The lad's mother was very upset about it at the time, but the boys made friends again.'

Bill Pegg was six months old when his family moved into the Brodsworth area of Yorkshire from Brampton, Derbyshire. They were of mining stock, and Bill became a banksman, responsible for the safety of the men travelling to and from the coal face in cages at Brodsworth Main colliery.

He worked at the colliery for forty-eight years and, just when the miners had won a better deal about pay and conditions, Bill had to leave the pit for health reasons.

Bill was pleased that England's football team was taking advantage of the talents of Liverpool left full back Alec Lindsay.

'That Lindsay's got real class,' he said. 'The way he passes a ball with that left foot of his and gets into such wonderful positions with such stylish movements. He's not one of those players who rushes everywhere and gets nowhere at the finish.

'The way he moves reminds me of Billy Whelan. I'm not a football expert and I'm just expressing my own opinion, but for me Billy Whelan would have been one of the greatest. He was one of the best I've ever seen. He would move with a slow gait, but he could do more with his feet than some could do with their hands.

'He used to delight me with his play. I would be mesmerized by his skill. I only spoke to him perhaps once. Billy was very shy. He used to stay with Mrs Watson in Manchester and she used to say to him "Why don't you go out with David, Billy? David's great for a night out."'

David was born at Highfields, in the house where his mother was born, and, like his father, his love affair with sport began in the depths of Highfields woods at a place known as 'The Hollow'.

Said father: 'We used to play all our sport down in The Hollow. When I was younger, and pennies and halfpennies were even harder to come by, we'd play "married versus singles" for a bob.

'One of our village sayings is "owt above ground has got to come down" and that's how we played it: hard. We'd use the trees as part of the game, playing off them. And if you hit a tree, well it was just a good defender! And we always had a case ball.'

Father used to play right half for local teams, including Highfields Institute, and in the cabinet, alongside his son's honours, are a couple of small silver cups of his own, the Doncaster Red Triangle, Division Two winner's Cup, 1933–4, and the Bentley Knock-out Trophy, 1934–5.

After the war he returned from the Middle East with a football and cricket bat he bought for David, and every spare moment, father and son would be out enjoying sport together. David, right-handed with a pen and a cricket bat, was a natural left-footed soccer player and developed his right foot kicking.

'I've always said that if a player is naturally stronger with either foot he will always prefer that foot,' said father. 'The only player I know of who was so good with either foot that he once took a penalty and could not say afterwards which foot he kicked the ball with was Cliff Bastin.

'The most famous footballer of them all did everything with his right foot. That was Stanley Matthews. But though David was naturally left-footed he was able to take corner kicks from either side and with either foot.'

David first played for Highfields Modern School, under the watchful eye of the headmaster Jim Boyle, and later passed an examination to go to Doncaster Technical School, where he continued his progress as an inside left.

'He was agile but thin,' said mother, 'and I'll always remember when he left to go to the Tech at thirteen because during the school holidays he broke an arm running into a wall playing a game called "husky-busky" with other children.

'David had just had the plaster off when his sports master asked if it would be all right for him to play football. The sports master was George Waite, who was on the Yorkshire Board of Selectors and was the one who later took him for a trial for England Boys.

'As far as his school work was concerned, he must have been all right to have passed for the Tech but we always used to joke about his school reports. It always used to say "steady" for all his subjects except sport when the marks were always higher than the rest.

'He used to grumble when he had to go to feed the hens we used to keep. But he'd take his dog – a wire-haired terrier called Spot – with him. One day Spot got run over and David cried like a baby.'

David continued to play inside left for Doncaster Boys, but Yorkshire Boys put him on the left wing, where he also played for England Under-fourteens and England Boys.

Father turned the pages of a photograph album and pointed to a picture of an England Boys team. 'You see that,' he said, 'there's Duncan Edwards, left half, and David, outside left, and that's how they went through life together. But when that picture was taken they didn't know they would both go to Manchester United.'

He thought again and added: 'I went to Oldham to watch David playing in a junior international match and spotted this chap in the crowd. I knew his face and he seemed to know mine, but I couldn't place him.

'I looked at him and he looked at me. Then suddenly he came to me and said "Mr Pegg, isn't it?" And he turned out to be my old sergeant major, Mr Norman Scholes, who was a schoolmaster and lived at Oldham.

'I told him I had come to watch David play and he said "Oh, what's he like?"

'"Oh, just so-and-so," I said.

'"Oh, so they're picking just so-and-sos for England now, are they?" he joked.

'After the match, he said "I like that so-and-so player of yours". And it just happened that with Mr Scholes that day was Bob Slater, the Manchester United scout. But that was a long time before David went to United.

'When the time came, he didn't need a great deal of

persuading because he always wanted to go to United. There have always been stories about what parents have got out of their boys joining a big football club and if I'm asked if I got anything out of it, I can always answer honestly and say yes.

'When David joined United he got the customary ten pounds signing on fee and said, "There you are dad, this is for you". That's what I got out of it.'

Said mother: 'Until he went to Manchester we always used to get David's studs from Woolworths in Doncaster and he used to be very particular about having hand-knitted football stockings.'

Said father: 'I remember we went to a shop in Doncaster to buy the boots that he took with him to Manchester and he had his feet x-rayed on a machine at the shop before he chose them.'

Upstairs were David's last pair of boots, the ones without studs he was bedding in by just walking on the soles. The ones he never got to wear on a football ground.

As a boy, David would play on Saturday mornings and go with his parents to watch Doncaster Rovers on Saturday afternoons. But his idol was a silver-haired inside forward who was the player-manager of Hull City, Raich Carter, the Sunderland, Derby County and England star, who later was also manager of Leeds United, Mansfield and Middlesbrough.

Like Carter, David played his first League game at seventeen, and in all played 127 First Division matches for United.

'They were all fine players at United,' said father, 'but David always liked Dennis Viollet as a player. They could read each other's play very well. Matt Busby saw me one time and said: "You never told me David could play inside forward, Bill. You know, he would make a good inside forward but I like him on the wing."

'David used to prefer inside forward, where he played at school. He always felt he could get more involved inside than on the wing, but I told him "You're all right where you are, it's the same price on the wing, lad".'

Said mother: 'David liked a joke when he was a boy, but he was never the boastful type.'

Father agreed: 'He was a bit like Bobby Charlton in some ways. He didn't go on about his football. He used to come home and say how he'd got on, but that was it.

'We used to love to go to Blackpool. Those were the best times, when the children were little. But one time David came with us when he was with United. We stayed at a boarding house and there wasn't much room, so David shared a room for the week with two other boys.

'Just before we left, one of the boys saw me and said, "Is that your son who's stayed with us?" I said it was and he went on: "We kept asking him what kind of work he did and he wouldn't tell us. That made us all the more curious but it took the whole week before he finally gave in and told us he played for Manchester United." That was typical of David. He had thought of being a draughtsman at one time but football always dominated his life.

'It was at Blackpool when David was younger that he was given some wonderful encouragement. He was training with England Boys there, and all the lads were asked what they considered to be their weaknesses.

'David said it was his right foot, so they put him over on the right and had him kicking the ball across. I think it was Bill Perry, the Blackpool player, who told David "I don't know about you having a weakness, you can hit the ball as hard as I can with your right foot".'

But David could be upset by criticism, as his father recalled: 'Players never need telling when they've had a poor game, and David was always the first to admit it himself. But he always looked at the papers.

'If we had been over to a match and he was coming back with us, he'd always try to get the football editions of the papers before we left.'

His mother said: 'If I'd been at a game, he'd always ask

how I thought he'd played because he knew I'd always tell him exactly what I thought.'

Said father: 'Yes, but if the football writers were having a go at him, he could be sensitive about it. But I used to tell him: "Ignore them, lad. They couldn't make a game of dominoes, never mind football."'

'A lot of the people who watch football are funny. It doesn't matter which ground you go to, there are always the moaners. I remember watching a game at Doncaster when Alick Jeffrey was playing and a fellow close to me hadn't a good word to say for him. He was just a big so-and-so with no ability according to him. Until Jeffrey scored with a brilliant header. Then the fellow said he was the greatest.'

His mother asked: 'Do you remember the time he had toothache at Tottenham?'

Father grimaced at the memory: 'The team had just got back from somewhere and David had been given an injection to kill the pain from the tooth. It made him ill.

'We were down for the match and we could see how sick David was when the team arrived. We didn't expect him to play, but there was no change when the team was announced and when the lads came out, two of them seemed to be keeping David up. They helped him to get ready in the dressing room.

'When the match started David didn't seem to know where he was and the first time he got the ball he set off running in the wrong direction. But the longer the game went on, the better he seemed to get. And he didn't have a bad game at the finish. We used to go to a lot of the matches but I was always working a seven-day week and, looking back, I wish I had been able to see more of the games.

'If it was an evening game I would have to leave early because I would be off to work again at four in the morning.'

The Peggs are hospitable, homely people, and David shared their open-door philosophy, entertaining his pals when he was a boy and team-mates when he became a professional footballer.

'Yes,' said his mother, 'our house used to be like a footballers' holiday camp, but those were wonderful times. He would always be bringing someone home with him. Sometimes three or four or even more.

'Tommy Taylor would come quite often, and he was great fun. The night before my daughter Doreen's wedding, Tommy and David arrived home late and had the girls making them chips in the early hours of the morning.

'That Tommy! One time when he came his hair was very very short. He had beautiful black, curly hair but it was tight against his head this time. One of the girls asked how much he'd asked the barber to take off, and Tommy said: "I just told him to keep cutting till it stopped raining".'

Said father: 'Tommy was a fine figure of a man. You didn't notice his physique so much when he was in a suit or even in football kit. But when he took his shirt off he was like Adonis.

'I remember being at Doncaster for a match one night and meeting Jimmy Murphy outside the ground. Jimmy and Matt Busby always used to say the three of us were alike – all miners.

'Jimmy said he'd been to a game at Barnsley and when I asked him if he fancied a player he said, "They've got an inside forward called Taylor. But I don't fancy him as an inside forward. I reckon he'll be the best centre forward in the country if he comes to United."

'When Tommy first arrived from the Second Division, it took him a while to adjust to the faster pace. But Jimmy Murphy was right.

'I remember when David got his first car, an old jalopy, he used to bring Bobby Charlton home. Bobby was in the army then. The three of us would go fishing.'

Said mother: 'When David would be at home he would go upstairs, pick out one of his favourite records, Sinatra or Nat

King Cole, turn the volume of his record player on full and take a bath.'

David had girl friends. 'He used to have a girl near home and then he had a girl friend in Manchester, who is now married. But nothing serious,' said mother.

Said father: 'One time David and some of the other lads from Mrs Watson's went to the pictures and missed their bus home. They ran back as fast as they could, but when they arrived Jimmy Murphy was sitting in the house. He put them right about keeping late hours.'

Said mother: 'Do you remember when he was accused of smoking?'

'Yes,' said father. 'David never smoked, but we heard that someone had said they saw him walking out with the team, smoking. It turned out that he had some kind of inhaler he was using to help clear his nose at the time and from a distance it looked just like a cigarette.

'One summer when Tommy Taylor was staying with us for a while, Tommy and David used to get up at seven in the morning, put on track suits and set off for a run. That was when they were supposed to be on holiday. That's how much those boys cared about their fitness.

'And often when he'd be home after playing for United on a Saturday, I'd see David on my way to work on Sunday having a kick around with some of the local lads.

'That was him. If there was a ball bouncing, he'd be bouncing. David won one full cap for England, but at the time he was playing, the great Stanley Matthews was on the right wing and the regular left winger was Tom Finney, as fine a player as ever put boots on.'

In the cabinet, with that cap, was an FA Cup Final medal, also from 1957. A runner's-up medal.

'We were at the banquet after that final,' recalled his mother, 'and I was just coming out of a lift when I saw Duncan Edwards. He must have thought by the look on my face that I was more upset than I was.'

'Yes,' said father. 'He started to look at his runner's-up medal and said, "I need that to complete my collection, because we'll be back with winners' medals next year".' Shortly before Munich, David, aged twenty-two, presented the 'David Pegg Cup' at a local school, and at St George's Church, Highfields, a carved chair at the side of the altar bears his name. At the other side of the altar is a similar chair dedicated to a boy who died in the Royal Air Force.

'The day of the funeral,' said his father, 'we were determined to be as composed as we possibly could as a family. We had done a lot of crying before that day, and wanted it to pass with as little fuss as possible.

'I had arranged for a playing of the footballers' anthem, "Abide With Me", because I thought that was appropriate. I knew that if mother could stand up to the day we would be all right, and before we started off I said "As soon as I open this door I want dry eyes until it is all over". We did the best we could. David would have wanted it that way.'

11. Tommy Taylor

'Tommy Taylor was the finest header of a ball I've seen. He suffered a lot from a bad ankle and took a lot of stick from the fans, but as far as the lads were concerned he was terrific. A player's player and a great person.'
DENNIS VIOLLET

'The Bog', a rock-hard piece of ground, sloping three different ways, with the tip of a boulder protruding eighteen inches in the middle, was the highest point of the Barnsley village of Smithies. It was also the home ground of Smithies United, where local boys played football in clogs, pit boots or bare feet and where weekends were a carefully planned routine. Saturday was filled with football, drinking, more football, more drinking, snooker and the pictures. Sunday was a repeat performance.

As a variation, the action would sometimes move to a second ground at the end of Richard Road, a pitch twenty yards long and ten yards wide, where they played games of ten goals change ends and fifteen-a-side 'marrieds versus singles'.

One day at The Bog, Smithies United were a man short and a lad from the pit strolling up to watch was greeted with the shout, 'Give us a game, Tommy!'

'Nay,' he replied. 'I've no clothes to play in.' But he was soon kitted out and joined in the match. Afterwards, much to his amazement, he was approached by two scouts who had been watching, one from Barnsley and the other from Hull City.

Both offered him trials, and Tommy Taylor chose Barnsley, where, as a groundstaff boy of fifteen, his wage packet was made out as shown below:

13 February 1948
Taylor, T.

Gross wages	£2 10s 0d
Nat. Ins. (H & P. Unem.)	£0 1s 11d
Special Fund	
Income Tax	
Wages less deductions	
Income Tax Refund	
Net amount	£2 8s 1d

It took explosives to force that boulder out of the middle of The Bog to make way for a pub called The Athersley that stands there now, with a magnificent picture of Tommy in the tap room.

One of the regulars is Harry England, Tommy's best friend, and a miner at North Gawber Colliery. Harry's brother, Alf, a former Barnsley and Mansfield Town winger and manager of Alfreton Town, is now secretary-director of Worksop Town. Another brother, Bob, is a miner at Dodworth Colliery. The three were bearers at Tommy's funeral.

But of all the England family, mother Margaret, now a grey-haired, grandmotherly figure, played the most prominent role in the life of young Tommy. She lives with her husband, Arthur, a retired miner also in his seventies, at the house in Richard Road that she said was 'like a second home to Tommy'.

It was a second home to the whole gang of Smithies, as Tommy's youngest brother, Bill, explained: 'There were about fifteen of us playing football and going around together at the time and Mrs England always had her door open to us.

'We used to go there to play cards and she would always have supper ready for us all when we came home from the pictures or the pub. But she would never have girls near the house.

'She really cared about us all and always had a soft spot for Tommy. If any of the boys was wanted at home, they only had to look in at Mrs England's to find him.'

Tommy used to do some show jumping for an ice cream vendor called Harry Kaye, who had a few horses.

'One day,' said Bill, 'we were in Harry Kaye's field, building up jumps about a foot high. Harry England ran, slipped, fell over the jump and smashed his knee cap. Tommy and I got him home in a wheelbarrow. Harry always had a limp after that. But he still played football, and the limp never deterred him.'

Tommy had a scar on his forehead from the day he fell off the mangle at his home, a two-up, one-down house at the back of a pub called The Woodman, run by his aunt Hester.

His brothers, Albert, Alex and Bill, and sisters Alice and Irene are still alive, though his mother, Violet, died a few years after Munich, and his father, Charles, who is in his late seventies and has lost his sight, lives at a local old people's home.

'Mother was the driving force from the start and kept all Tommy's newspaper cuttings in a scrapbook right from the time he was playing for the schoolboys,' said Bill.

'She was a wonderful woman who would stand for no nonsense. I remember making a nuisance of myself one day when she had a big plate in her hand. In the end I goaded her by saying, "Go on, then, hit me with that plate". Next thing I knew my hand hurt and the two halves of the plate were either side of me on the table.'

Bill carries a newspaper cutting of his own in his wallet. It praises him as 'another Taylor' and offers the opinion of the judge who wrote the piece that 'Bill could become even greater than his brother'.

It did not work out that way, as Bill explained: 'I was a centre half, but I carried a lot of weight and I was only about five feet six as a youngster. Later I got taller and slimmed down so that I was more Tommy's build (six feet tall and about twelve-and-a-half stone).

'But in my early days I would put on a stone every year, so that when I was eleven I would be eleven stone, when I was twelve, twelve stone, and so on. I didn't let too many forwards past me, but when they went I had a job catching them. But I had two short spells at Barnsley.

'Later I received a bad injury. The ligaments went in my knee. I was working in the pit at the time, and never thought too much about a football career after that.' Bill now runs a local bakery with his wife, Audrey, who is a director. He believes his son, Tommy's nephew, Ian Thomas, aged ten, should be the next generation of the footballing Taylors. 'My grandfather, Tommy, played centre half for Barnsley when it was the original club, Barnsley St Peter's. And my father was a centre half, too.

'He was offered a trial with Wakefield Trinity, which was a top soccer team of the time. But when he was on his way to catch the bus to go to show Wakefield what he could do, some of his mates were outside a pub and called him over for a drink for luck. He never got there in the end.

'But our uncle Tommy was a centre half, I was a centre half and, of course, Tommy was a centre forward. It should be Ian's turn now, and he's always shown an aptitude for the game. He's got the natural ability even though he's a bit on the chubby side like I was.

'The only thing is, Ian doesn't seem particularly keen on the game. He's the same about rugby at his school. The teacher told me he was as good a rugby player as they had got when he wanted to play, but he didn't always want to play.'

Tommy and Bill attended Raley Secondary Modern School, Barnsley, which Bill claimed 'bred men and sportsmen but not intellectuals. If you wanted them you had to go to the Grammar School.'

He added: 'Raley was a great school, very well equipped with a superb gym and its own swimming pool. It was very good for sports. Arthur Rowe, the shotputter, and Dickie Bird, the Test umpire, and a whole string of lads who became professional footballers and class cricketers went to Raley.

'There was a girls' section and a boys' section, and the girls' choir sang on the radio.

'The Taylors were more average than bright, but we were not fools, all the same. Our marks were pretty good. We were in the "A" classes.

'Tommy didn't get into fights. We were not an aggressive family. Tommy in particular was very placid most of the time, though he did have a violent temper if it was brought out, which took some doing.

'I could always tell when he got mad when he was playing. He used to clench his fists and grit his teeth to ease the tension building up inside him.

'We were all pretty athletic and we'd never open the gate at home. We always vaulted the hedge, very careful that we cleared it, because anyone who touched it had to clip it.

'But we had a way of standing, a sort of footballer's slouch, with a hand in a pocket and a generally relaxed posture that took inches off our true heights.'

Said Bill's wife, Audrey: 'And you both walked pin-toed, a real flick-footed footballer's walk.

'And I can remember times when Tommy would come home and have an injury and his mother would rub his leg with horse liniment.'

When fifteen years old, Tommy walked 'pin-toed' into Barnsley Football Club. Inside forward Johnny Steele was then a club coach and has now served Barnsley for almost forty years as player, coach, manager, general manager and secretary. He took a break from wrestling with Value Added Tax to recall:

'When Tommy arrived here he did all the jobs groundstaff boys used to do, cleaning boots and working on the ground.

And he loved it. He wouldn't go home. We had to kick him off the ground.

'He was a great practical joker. He would turn the cold hose on you or hide your shoes and you had to watch out when it was Guy Fawkes' night because all day he'd be throwing squibs around you.

'Tommy always had a happy, cheeky, laughing face. He was full of life. That was the real tragedy.

'We didn't have a youth team then. We used to play friendly games at youth level and later, under the guidance of chairman Mr Joe Richards, we started the Northern Intermediate League, and Tommy played in that.

'Angus Seed was the manager then, but as the coach, I saw a lot of Tommy.

'He always looked an outstanding player, and his brother, Bill, was a good player too. In fact, if anything he was better with the ball on the ground than Tommy, though he didn't have Tommy's other great assets.

'Bill came down a few times, but he tended to put on weight and didn't stay long. Tommy was chubby in those days. At fifteen he carried quite a lot of puppy fat, and I thought it might be the one thing that could handicap him. But National Service made all the difference. He shot up and slimmed down.

'He played for the British Army and was in our reserves. But towards the end of his National Service he got into our first team and I used to nip over to his camp in North Wales to fetch him home on Friday nights.

'During his time in the army he got a bad knee injury in a tackle during one of their games. It was ligament trouble, but he got over it. He was the best header of a ball in the game, what I call a positive header. He would always make use of the ball in the air.

'If he was too far out to have an effective header at goal, he would look around for the man in the best position to nod it on to. And he could hang in the air while he thought about it. Not many could do that.

'He had a great shot in either foot – he could murder a ball – but tended to be a bit clumsy on the ball.

'At one stage he got a bit top-heavy. He was always an exuberant lad, but he became a bit cheeky. People began to think he was big-headed, but he was never really that even though he did start giving backchat. You had to know him to understand him.

'Tommy could upset people by letting them know how he felt, and he himself could be upset by criticism. He would say what others might only think. There was one time when Angus Seed upset him over something, and Tommy gave him a bit of a mouthful. And the relationship between Tommy and Eddie McMorran became a little strained at times.

'Eddie was a great individualist rather than a team man. He loved to beat men and would often use a team-mate to do it. An opponent, knowing another player was in a position to take a pass from Eddie, would be wavering. Eddie would keep nodding towards the team-mate, who would be bursting to get the ball. But Eddie would then dribble past the opponent.

'This would happen a lot, and some of the lads found the habit infuriating. And, as usual, Tommy would speak his mind.

'It takes a special type to become a good forward. You may have a half back who is great moving forward with the ball and be tempted to put him into the attack. But it's a different game up there. You start with your back towards the target and with men at your back. You've got to turn before you can start.

'A special skill is needed for this. I remember Danny Blanchflower upfield at Barnsley. They thought he would make a great inside forward but, wonderful half back that he was, he never got a kick at the ball up front.

'Tommy scored a lot of goals for us, and he got over that

spell when people thought he was getting a bit above himself. I've never yet met the perfect person. We all have faults and people are always quick to take to pieces those who manage to get to the top.'

When Tommy was twenty, Second Division Barnsley were visited by seventeen League clubs all wanting to take him to the top and it seemed only a matter of time before the then record fee of £35,000 paid by Sheffield Wednesday to Notts County for Jackie Sewell would be smashed.

Wednesday eventually declared themselves not interested in paying a fee of around £30,000 for Tommy. And one by one, other clubs dropped out of the chase, Derby County, Wolves, Cardiff.

But one day in March 1953, Tommy left the home of Mrs England and went to the Royal Hotel, Barnsley, to talk terms with Manchester United.

He signed at a transfer fee of £29,999 – United did not want him to carry a £30,000 price tag.

'Tommy never wanted to leave Barnsley at all,' said Johnny Steele. 'And we didn't want him to go. But he had to, for financial reasons. The club needed the money. They could have made more money from selling Tommy than they did, but Mr Richards had given Matt Busby his word that United would have first refusal, and he didn't go back on his word.

'I heard locally that Jimmy Murphy watched Tommy seventeen times before he was satisfied United should make their move for him.

'It was a big thing for Tommy to go to Manchester. It's always hard at first for a boy from a small town to go to a city club. But he went at the right time because he was beginning to get in with a drinking crowd and he was the local hero, a good-natured lad who was rather easily led then.

'He settled down quickly at Old Trafford, but he used to come back here to see us and to tell us how things were going for him.'

Said brother Bill: 'It was hard for Tommy because he was

leaving all his mates and going somewhere completely new and different, but it was a great opportunity for him and he took it well.'

Tommy scored 112 goals in 168 League appearances with United and, with nineteen full caps, had become England's top centre forward. His heading ability was supreme and, as Steele said, he could 'murder' a ball with either foot. He would also run miles to aid his team-mates.

But with the ball at his feet he still gave the impression of a man who felt he never had enough time in which to pack the hundred and one things he wished to do on a football field.

'Yes, he could look a bit clumsy at times,' said Steele, 'and I know Henry Rose, for one, had his reservations about Tommy. But the boy more than made up for his anxious ball control with his other tremendous abilities.

'No one taught Tommy how to play. He was a natural. United always looked after their players and they always played to their strengths. Their play was not all off the cuff, but they never curbed individualism.

'I remember when people started talking about twin centre forwards. Tommy told me of the time he was on tour with England, when Walter Winterbottom was in charge. Walter decided to use Tommy and Nat Lofthouse as his twins and told one player to take the far post and the other to go for the near post when the ball was ready to be crossed.

'But this is where instinctive play takes over. Tommy and Nat both went for the far post and ended up knocking each other over.'

Tommy rarely let his anger rise to the surface, though Peter Thomas, then Northern Sports Editor of the *Daily Mirror*, recalled: 'Once, only once, did he act in retribution – against Real Madrid at Old Trafford, when the tempers of the crowd and players were red hot after a tackle on Taylor by Marquitos, a centre half with the shoulders of an ox and the finesse of one of the original railway navvies.

'Tommy suffered one or two more ferocious tackles in silence, and then, as a long centre came over, went for the ball in the air ... and got it *and* Marquitos just where he wanted them. But, mark it well, he got the ball.'

Former Huddersfield Town footballer and Yorkshire cricketer Ken Taylor was the man Tommy named as the hardest centre half he had played against. Returning the compliment in full, Ken, who left Huddersfield in 1965, stopped playing first class cricket in 1968 and is now teaching art at Gresham's School, Norfolk, after spending a few years in South Africa, said:

'I played against the biggest names of the time – Nat Lofthouse, Jackie Milburn, Stan Mortensen, Trevor Ford, Ronnie Allen, Dave Hickson, Dennis Wilshaw, Don Revie and Billy Liddell – and Tommy was the best.

'He was so tremendous in the air, a great two-footed player, fast, manoeuvrable and did so much work. He would be on one wing one minute and the other the next.

'We both played it very hard, though he usually came off the better. We never did play well against United. I knew Tommy as a person as well as an opponent and he was a great chap. We chatted on the field. There were no hard feelings.

'He was also keen on cricket and used to come to see me when Yorkshire played Lancashire at Old Trafford.'

Tommy was right-handed in most things, but was a left-hander at both cricket and golf.

'He liked a Guinness,' said brother Bill. 'So do I, though I only touch a drink on the odd occasions I go out now. We did some boozing when we were young, because lads were brought up on beer round here. But Tommy put football above everything.

'I remember my bachelor party on 3 February 1957. It was a Wednesday and six of us went to a pub in Barnsley and Tommy was the only one who didn't have a drink. He was on tonic water and Lucozade all the time.

'There was a raffle and Tommy bought one ticket and was then asked to make the draw. He drew his own ticket ... but they wouldn't hand over the £5 prize!

'Next day I got married at 11.00 a.m. and at 1.00 p.m. Tommy had to leave the reception at the Queen's Hotel, Barnsley, to catch a train to Blackpool where United were having special training before a game against Real Madrid.'

Bill keeps what is left of Tommy's collection of caps, medals and trophies in a cabinet tucked away for safety's sake in a 'glory-hole' at his home. 'A lot of the stuff has gone, taken from time to time by people who used to come round for a look when the cabinet was at my parents' house,' he said.

There is the strip Tommy wore against Aston Villa in the 1957 FA Cup Final, still stained with Wembley turf, though only because Audrey was restrained from washing it one day. Bill said that one day he intended to offer the contents of the cabinet to Barnsley Corporation to be put on public view.

Bill and Audrey talked of Tommy's fiancée, Carol, a Manchester girl now married and living in the south of England. 'It was a long time before Carol began to recover from Munich,' said Audrey.

'They were a great crowd of lads and girls in those days,' said Bill. 'The players might have seemed reserved, but when they got together they could really enjoy themselves amongst themselves.'

He played one of Tommy's favourite records, Kay Starr singing 'Wheel of Fortune', and said Tommy also liked the Platters and Benny Goodman and had a fairly wide range of tastes.

'I think I got on well with him because I knew nothing about football, though I'm mad about it now,' said Audrey. 'It didn't show on the outside, but I always felt Tommy was a bit unsure of himself. He was always trying to improve himself and thinking of the future. He wanted to set me up in business as a hairdresser, but I told him I was already committed with the bakery.

'He used to ask me the best way to approach certain things. And when we went round to his digs in Manchester to collect his things, we found two little black and yellow books, *Teach Yourself Public Speaking* and *Teach Yourself Maths*. It broke my heart when I saw those because they showed just how much he wanted to improve himself.'

Said Bill, 'Tommy used to say he would rather be dead than not be able to play football, so in a way I suppose it was a blessing that he did not come out of that crash alive but so badly maimed that he would not have been able to play or enjoy life. You see, he loved football and he loved life, did our Tom.'

12. Liam Whelan

'Liam Whelan was a great player. He had everything except an extra bit of pace. When I got into the side it was at Liam's expense but he would have been back because he was a dedicated professional with a tremendous amount of skill.'
BOBBY CHARLTON

The shy young Dubliner, newly arrived at Old Trafford, was greeted by a famous countryman, Manchester United captain Johnny Carey, who asked: 'And what's your name, then?'

'Liam,' said the boy.

'Liam, is it?' said Carey with a smile. 'Well, hold on to it as long as you can. They're sure to take it away from you here!'

Sure enough, to most Mancunians the tall, immensely talented Irish boy was, and is, known as Billy Whelan.

'I called him William, after my father,' said Mrs Elizabeth Whelan, 'but my husband did not want him to be called William, so we settled for the Irish version, Liam.'

John Whelan, who died in 1943, aged forty-two, when the son destined to be famous was still a mere street and schoolyard footballer, would have been proud to see the name of his choice perpetuated in Dublin.

There is the 'Liam Whelan Cup' at school sports in Phibsboro, the 'Liam Whelan Youth Club' in his own home district of Cabra, and even a football team, 'Liam Whelan United', playing in a local schoolboy league.

Liam's subtle skills at inside right or centre forward were so rare that United received an approach from Brazil, an offer of riches and fame, after his performance in a youth tournament in Switzerland.

His way of life, clearly defined, uncomplicated and based on a deep religious conviction, is still held up as an example to the youth of Ireland by members of the clergy who knew him well.

But Liam was the last man to thrust his name forward or make loud noises about his success. In fact he worried that people might think him boastful, and whenever he wore a United club blazer he would hold a raincoat over an arm in a way that would hide the badge so he would not appear to be showing off.

He was never happier than when he was at home with his family, brothers Christy and John and sisters Alice, Maura and Rita.

Like Liam, Christy and John were both well known in local football. They followed their father's example, for John Whelan, a strong man who stood six feet two inches, played for Brunswick and Strandville, won junior cup medals and was reckoned to be the best centre half in junior football.

He signed forms for League of Ireland club Drumcondra, but never got around to playing for them because he regretted leaving his pals and went back to rejoin them in junior football.

John junior, a fireman with two children, John and Gillian, did play for Drumcondra – for six years in fact. He started as an inside forward, then reverted to full back, and, in 1968, Manchester United packed Dalymount Park when they played in his testimonial match.

Christy, a time-keeper at the Special Works Department of Dublin Corporation, with four children, Brigid, Deirdre, Hilda and Christopher, was an inside forward or wing half. He played one season for Drumcondra and seven seasons for Transport, when they were a League of Ireland team.

Alice, Mrs Alice Burke, has five children, Elizabeth, Carol, Geraldine and twin boys, Michael and Eamonn. Maura, Mrs

Maura Collins, has four children, Liam, Anthony, Marie and Bernadette.

Liam, thirteen, named after his famous uncle, and Anthony, ten, have followed the family tradition of playing organized football with Dublin's Home Farm club, a nursery for so many Republic of Ireland stars. They were both members of junior teams and Anthony was preparing in 1974 for a semi-final of the club's mini-league, as a forward, for 'Southampton' against 'Manchester City'.

Said his grandmother: 'Anthony is most like Liam in looks, even to the freckles.'

Anthony used to idolize George Best but switched his allegiance to United's captain, Willie Morgan.

Rita Whelan, Liam's other sister, is unmarried and works at a local biscuit factory. She takes a keen interest in football and, like the rest of the family, was greatly saddened when United were relegated.

The Whelans were born and reared at St Attracta Road, Cabra, where Mrs Whelan and Rita still live.

'Liam used to spend his days out there on the road playing football with the rest of the boys from around here,' said his mother, 'and then he used to play football in the Corporation playground.

'They had a team they called the Red Rockets, and Liam was captain.

'The Red Rockets used to travel all over Dublin playing football in other Corporation playgrounds. Mr McIntyre, an attendant at the playground, used to encourage the boys a lot in those days.

'Yes, the boys used to have great fun playing in the playgrounds and in the street, God bless them. You don't see the boys playing out there now and I'm sure they'd be a lot better off if they did.'

Liam attended St Peter's School, Phibsboro, where the windows looked out over Dalymount Park, home of Bohemians and the Republic of Ireland international team.

Said Christy: 'Even though Dalymount was right next to the school and just over the bridge from our home, Liam was never keen on watching football when he was young. He only went to watch with a group of lads from Home Farm if there was something special on, or to see Paddy Coad playing for Shamrock Rovers.

'Paddy, the Rovers' inside forward, was Liam's favourite player. Paddy was reckoned to be the most famous Irish player never to go across to play for an English club. He would always be the player Liam would go to see.'

At St Peter's, Liam won medals for Gaelic football and hurling, and one of his hurling team-mates was Joe Carolan, who later joined United as a defender.

'Once Liam was picked to play for Dublin at Gaelic football and hurling on the same day,' said Christy. 'He decided to go for the football.'

Said mother: 'At a certain age, Liam had to choose between Gaelic games and soccer, and he chose soccer. It was his whole life.'

'Yes,' said Christy. 'He would never talk about anything else when he was young. Like most boys his age, he would sooner be playing football than be sitting at school. Mr O'Shea was his sports master, and was a great influence on Liam at school.

'Liam was never any trouble at school. He sometimes got into fights with other boys, the way boys do, but there were never any complaints about his behaviour.'

Said mother: 'Father Allen was the school's spiritual director, and he was a good influence on Liam. Father Allen still speaks about Liam, the way he lived and that sort of thing.'

In 1951, Liam played for a Republic of Ireland schoolboy international team that beat England 8–4, and when he joined Home Farm in his early teens, his career was guided by Tom Smith and Charlie Jackson. Christy and his brother-in-law, Michael, became Liam's biggest supporters.

'When Liam played football on Saturdays, we changed to

playing on Sundays so that we could watch him,' said Christy, 'and when he was playing on Sundays we moved back to playing Saturdays.

'There was one particular player who gave Liam more trouble than most as a junior in Dublin. That was Brendan McNally, the centre half who went to Luton Town.'

Said mother: 'After a match, Liam would come into the house and I would ask him how the team had done. "Oh, we won," he would say. And I would ask him how he had played. "Oh, fair," he would say. I'd have to wait for Christy to come in to tell me exactly how he had played.'

Said Christy: 'I used to marvel at Liam's skill with a ball and it always puzzled me that he was never approached by a League of Ireland club. I know he was my brother, but even in those days, I thought he was one of the best prospects I'd ever seen in Ireland.'

Manchester United signed Liam when he was eighteen. They needed a replacement for injured inside forward John Doherty in time for the FA Youth Cup Final against Wolves in 1953.

Bert Whalley travelled to Dublin to try to sign Liam's Home Farm team-mate Vinny Ryan, usually a wing half, who had just returned from an international youth tournament in Belgium, where he had moved to centre forward and scored a hat-trick in a 3–2 win against Luxembourg. Liam was also on that tour.

The Home Farm senior team had a match on the Thursday night, and Whalley went to watch, along with Billy Behan, United's chief scout in Southern Ireland. Watching the match, Bert Whalley said he would like the boy Whelan immediately.

After playing for Home Farm on the Thursday, Liam arrived in Manchester the following Monday, signed amateur forms, became a full-time professional within a week, and, nine days after his move, starred in a 7–1 win over Wolves in the first leg of the final.

Said mother: 'When Billy Behan came to see us about Liam going over to Manchester, he said: "Well, if he never makes it I won't have lost a friend" and indeed, Billy has been a great friend of the family ever since.'

Said Christy: 'Liam never let us down in any way. No matter where he went, he would never put himself above anyone else. If he came over for a match, he loved to see all his old friends and would always join in whatever they were doing.

'He was always the same with his friends. You would never be afraid to ask "Would you do this, Liam?" or "Would you do that, Liam?" And though he was quiet, he had a good sense of humour and loved a joke.'

'Yes,' said mother, 'he was the biggest villain under the sun for creating fun.'

Said Christy: 'As a boy he was a great practical joker and when he went to United he had some great laughs.

'He told me about one time when the team stayed at Blackpool, at a hotel where each room had a special noise device for awakening guests, which Eddie Colman had arranged to go off in the early hours of the morning. Liam enjoyed the joke immensely.

'The Irish boys used to look up to Liam at United because he set them a good example. Boys like Joe Carolan, Johnny Giles and Jackie Mooney. Liam had a car, a real old banger that used to stop without warning.

'Liam was driving some of the boys down Deansgate in Manchester and the car kept stopping. Out they would get, give the car a shove and then run to jump in before the engine stopped again. This happened a few times, but the car kept stalling on them.

'In the end, when they had pushed yet again and the engine came to life, Liam left them all standing and drove right around the block to make sure it kept going. When he passed them the second time around, he slowed down so that they could jump in without him having to stop.

'That car! When Liam died I came to Manchester and was

using it. A friend, Sean Doran, was with me. We were stopped by a policeman who started to inspect the car. He found fault with almost everything about it and took his notebook out and asked, "Who does the car belong to?"

'Sean told him, "Well, it was Liam Whelan's . . ." and he put his book away and said, "Oh, that's all right then . . . but I wouldn't drive it again if I were you".

'Liam used to ring me up and ask when I was coming over to Manchester. I used to go seven or eight times a year. Sometimes I wouldn't even let Liam know I was coming.'

Liam won four senior caps for the Republic of Ireland, against Holland, Denmark, and two matches against England, losing 5–1 at Wembley and drawing 1–1 at Dalymount.

Christy recalled the England game at Dalymount: 'Liam had a favourite trick of pushing the ball between an opponent's legs, and before the game with England Duncan Edwards bet Liam he couldn't do that to him.

'Well, during the game Liam got the ball on a touchline and when Duncan came to tackle, sure enough he pushed the ball through Duncan's legs. As Liam moved away, Duncan rapped his ankle and the crowd gave a roar of disapproval. But it was unintentional. Duncan was not the type to do that sort of thing on purpose.'

Liam's sister Alice remembered: 'We were all proud of him playing for United and once when he was home I said to him, "Oh, it's great to think of you playing for United", and he said, "Ah, but it could end tomorrow".' Said Christy: 'Liam loved to come home. He used to say sometimes he wished his football career was over and he could come back and start a little business. When he came home he hated a fuss.

'We went to watch a match at Dalymount one day and it wasn't long before a group of thirty to forty boys gathered round Liam asking for autographs. He signed the autographs but that didn't seem to be enough and he felt the fuss was disturbing the men around us who were watching the match. So, he said to me, "I'm off, I'll see you at home".'

On the sideboard at mother's home in St Attracta Road are all the trophies won by members of the Whelan family, including Liam's Gaelic medals.

Mother went to a cabinet and brought out an artificial red rose in a plastic box. 'Liam brought me this to cheer me up when I had just had a big operation,' she said. 'It was the last present he ever brought me.

'Liam used to be in great form when he came home for a holiday. He used to go out into the road and give the toddlers some money to buy a ball, and then he would join in their game.'

Said Christy: 'He was over with United to play in a five-a-side tournament involving eight professional teams. The afternoon before the tournament he was out in the road playing football with some of the neighbours' children and he scored three goals. One of the players on his side was a little girl called Nora. That night he scored three goals in the tournament and when he came home he said to her: "That's not bad . . . two hat-tricks in the same day!"

'Two weeks after United lost to Aston Villa in the 1957 Cup Final, Liam interrupted a holiday in Kilkenny to join his pals in Killester for United's seven-a-side tournament.

'Our team was called Frank's Boys after Frank Roe, who was the manager. When we were getting ready for the first round we were short of a goalkeeper and straight away Liam volunteered for the job. I said, "No, Liam, I'll go in goal. You play outfield where you will be of more benefit to the team." We won the tournament and it was mainly due to Liam.'

Liam played his first League game for United in the 1954–5 season and scored 43 goals in 79 League matches before he died in his twenty-third year.

Said mother: 'When he first went to Manchester he lived at Mrs Watson's and then he moved to other digs at Mrs Gibb's.'

Said Christy: 'He was great pals with Bobby Charlton and they shared the same room for a time. Bobby and Liam were the types who would take whatever clothes were nearest to them in the mornings no matter who they belonged to. They wore each other's clothes and never thought anything about it.

'Liam used to collect records. He liked Perry Como, Guy Mitchell and Frank Sinatra and he used to swap records with David Pegg.

'But Liam was happiest during his last two years over in Manchester. Sean Doran, a football friend of ours who played for Bohemians, had a brother, Brendan, who was the manager of Louis Edwards' canning factory and lived near Stockport.

'Sean got in touch with Brendan and fixed it up for Liam to move in with his family. It was really home from home for Liam there.'

Said mother: 'And one of Liam's great friends in Manchester was Father Mulholland, the parish priest of St Sebastian's. Father Mulholland looked after the Irish boys who lived in Manchester and he was very good to Liam.'

Said Christy: 'Due to this relationship and his good way of living, there were rumours that Liam was going to become a priest and he was asked about this shortly before Wembley in 1957. He told the reporters "Not at all. I'm going to be married."'

Added mother: 'Liam was planning to be married in the June of 1958 to a friend of the family who has since married and lives in Dublin.'

Liam, or William, or Billy. The name has not been forgotten.

'I've had hundreds of nice letters from people who knew Liam in Manchester, telling me all about him,' said mother, 'and three girl supporters I have never met still send money for flowers and send me lovely cards.

'We've made wonderful friends in Manchester and Matt Busby and everyone else at United have been very good to us. Very understanding.'

149

Alice added: 'Mother has even had a letter from a priest in Spain to tell her what Liam had done to help the boys in his town, sending old football shirts and things like that.'

Said Christy: 'I always remember watching United run out for matches, with Roger Byrne coming up the tunnel and dropping the ball on his foot and kicking it up to his head. They always looked so confident in those red shirts.

'I went to see United's FA Cup semi-final against Fulham in 1958 and when the team came out and I saw the number eight shirt, worn that day by Ernie Taylor, I was a bit overcome.

'Some people feel it is better to forget the past. But we don't want to forget. We love talking about Liam.'

Said mother: 'Harry Gregg saw us after the crash and told us what Liam had said just before it happened. Those words have been a great comfort to us ever since.'

The words were: 'If the worst happens, I am ready for death. I hope we all are.'

13. The Press Team

Another team was on board the Elizabethan, a group of journalists who had shared and recorded the progress of 'The Babes' and other sporting greats of the 1950s. Sometimes their writings reflected a critical eye. Sometimes their reports were spiced with good humour. Often they would speculate about the boundless potential of the young United players.

Frank Taylor of the *News Chronicle* survived a nightmare experience that will live with him for ever, but happily he was soon able to continue his career and later joined the *Daily Mirror*. His colleagues perished, and the loss to journalism was equal at least to the loss to football.

In newspaper offices throughout Manchester on 6 February 1958, sports departments awaited the return of their reporters with follow-up stories on United's progress into the semi-finals of the European Cup. Instead came news of the crash.

What it was like that day is told here by men who were friends and colleagues of those who would never write again.

The story must have been similar in every office. Bill Fryer, of the *Daily Express*, recalls the scene in Great Ancoats Street, Manchester: 'It was around three o'clock in the afternoon as near as memory takes me. I was preparing Henry Rose's postbag, a job he always invited me to do when he was away on his travels.

'I don't think Henry had really been looking forward to this one. He hadn't been too well, and he wasn't his usual sparkling self when we discussed the coming trip a few days before.

'It was around three and I had just typed the catchline "Postbag 1".

'The *Daily Express* editorial room in the Manchester office, large, spacious, with its million telephones and billion type-writers clattering and ringing only spasmodically, was still in the calm of afternoon's expectations before the breeze, storm or gale of the evening's happenings, which nightly can become any of the three.

'Subeditors were few about the place, since there was not yet much to subedit. Copytakers tapped away at the early stuff, greyhounds, racing cards and what not. A backbencher or two read copy. No serious scheming of layouts yet. All very quiet and clerical – not a bit like anybody's idea of a newspaper as depicted by Hollywood.

'We on sport had something to work on, with such things as horse-racing demanding many statistics. I can't remember exactly who of us was there at the time. I can see Eric Cooper, in charge, working away at his racing make-ups, his diary and schedules stacked neatly in his mind of a million pigeon-holes, which housed knowledge of any sport you could care to mention. Little Archie (Thompson) chirruped his inevi-table repertoire of racing deletions and the deficiencies of current messenger boys compared with the time, thirty-odd years before, when he himself had been head lad.

'Our own messenger, Brian Gledhill, was excepted from Archie's chamber of horror-boys, being inordinately and precociously gifted at horse-racing and its complexities and therefore a help to Archie.

'All, indeed, was calm.

'Then came a flash, an agency flash.

'"Manchester United aircraft crashed on take-off," it said, as near as I can remember it.

'All chatter stopped. But perhaps it wasn't too bad. The aircraft may not have been far off the ground since it was in take-off.

'But minutes later came another flash ... "Heavy loss of life feared". I am pretty sure those were the exact words.

'Suddenly nobody sat. Nobody stood still. Everybody seemed to be moving about. Just pacing about as if ready to leap to somebody's help. Who was dead? It just didn't bear thinking about. I myself knew almost everybody on that aircraft, journalistic colleagues, Matt Busby, Walter Crickmer, the players. Yes, the players. They were only kids, most of them. Who was dead? We daren't ask.

'In came David Nicholls, Eric Cooper's deputy. He had heard something on the radio. It was his day off but he couldn't keep away. He thought the same as the rest of us. What can we do?

'One thing we had to do was to produce a paper about the biggest story in my time as far as England's and particularly Manchester's emotions have been concerned.

'When Neville Chamberlain told the nation that war had been declared, my wife cried. She cried because she didn't know what was going to happen to us. At six o'clock on the afternoon of 6 February 1958, Eric Cooper cried. He cried as he schemed the pages, pictures of all the players, copy about everybody. We all worked like maniacs, as if first we were doing something for the victims and second producing a newspaper.

'I have seen many hard-bitten newspapermen as cold-looking as codfish in face of the most blood-curdling stories. I saw no cold-looking newspapermen that night.

'The names of the victims came, spasmodically, every name a stab in the heart. "It can't be. I was with him only last week," as if no such awful thing could happen on that account.

'For once inter-office rivalry was forgotten. Office rang office. Any news of Henry? Any news of George? What about Alf? As if any one of us had some secret source that could spew the frightful worst or breathe the relieving best.

'"No. Not young Colman." I could see little Eddie shaking

a hip and wriggling past an opponent now. "No, not young Colman" and "No, not Tommy Taylor." I had never seen the lad without a smile on his face. That face in a smashed-up plane was unimaginable.

'"No, not Roger Byrne." "No, not big Mark Jones." "No, not Geoff Bent." "No, not perky young David Pegg." "No, not that shy lad Liam Whelan. How could this happen to him? He never harmed anybody, not even an opponent."

'"Poor old Alf Clarke. He watched United so often that when a Red was kicked Alf limped." "And dear old Tom Jackson. Never harmed anyone in his life." "Neither did Eric Thompson. He'd help anybody."

'"No, not George Follows. How could a talent like that be wiped out? What a waste."

'And dear old Archie Ledbrooke. Always burning his hand on my cigarette when we were on the old *Daily Dispatch.* "You should start smoking, Archie," I used to say to him. "Smokers never burn their hands on other people's cigarettes." Archie did a lot for me. I hope I did a little for him. Yes, I'd burned his hands. But now, this day, I wish he were here to burn them again.

'"How's Big Dunc?" "He's injured. So's Matt. So are Johnny Berry and Jackie Blanchflower. We don't know how badly yet." "So's Frank Taylor." "Poor old Swifty's gone."

'"It looks as if Bobby Charlton, Bill Foulkes, Albert Scanlon, Harry Gregg and Dennis Viollet are OK."

'"Any news about Henry yet?" "Why haven't we heard about Henry?" "Yes we have. Henry's dead."

'"Are the captions for the victim pictures down yet?"

'"No, not Henry." "He can't be. I was just preparing his postbag," as if that was protection enough. "How can Henry die? That's his chair. How can it be a chair without Henry in it? Can't imagine it."

'The good turns Henry did for fellow journalists were boundless. But trust Henry to go out in the most dramatic way even he could have chosen. In the line of duty for his beloved *Daily Express*. And with the biggest splash of even his massive turnout in over thirty years as sports editor.

'"How are the obits going?"

'"Any other victims?" "Yes, old Tom Curry and Walter Crickmer and Bert Whalley. Where can you find three like those? Every one a gentleman."

'The chat went on among the work for once. If a man couldn't pace about but had to sit, he had to chatter. Nobody wanted to be left alone with his silence. Too many memories that were yet hardly memories, as if we half expected Henry to stride through the door with his own story of the crash ready to type.

'The typewriters clattered and the phones shrilled impatiently. There is no such article as a patient-sounding telephone.

'Then all was done that could be done for the first run. There they were. All the names, all the pictures, all the words.

'It was true then. We were convinced now. We had produced the paper, but it had taken our own paper to convince us. There it was in black and white.

'"That looks like Henry lying there in the white shirt." We never really found out whether it was Henry or not. But we did not expect him to stride into the office any more.

'Then more stuff, re-jigs, ads, more pictures, more chatter. Midnight came. One o'clock in the morning came. Bill Sarson, from the Woodcourt pub, came. He had served the United players in a previous pub. Why did he come into the office? He didn't seem to know. Disbelief I think. It is hard to believe what you don't want to believe. He was in his carpet-slippers, yet the Woodcourt was miles out of town.

'Two o'clock came. Time to go home. I don't know anybody who went home. To the Press Club. To the Cromford Club. How could you go home? I suppose the feeling was that if something so gigantically awful as this could happen something else was bound to happen.

'As far as I was concerned I must have a drink. Everybody

decided he must have a drink. We all did go home. The milkman arrived at the same time.

'And every night for two weeks nobody seemed to want to go home. Matt was fighting for his life. So was Duncan Edwards. Johnny Berry was dreadfully injured. Jackie Blanchflower was badly injured.

'The end of the beginning of this came on the fifteenth day following the crash. Big Dunc, the indestructible, had lost his fight. Big Dunc, the boy who was a man at fifteen. Probably the most valuable player who ever kicked a ball for one team. Not money value alone. Sheer value. If ever one player was as useful as two ordinary mortals in a team, that player was Dunc.'

Eric Cooper, former northern sports editor of the *Daily Express*, remembers his friend Henry Rose: 'It is doubtful whether there was ever a more enigmatic character in newspaper journalism than Henry, who was probably better known to friends and foes – be they competitors, journalists or readers – than any other writer in the sporting field.

'Henry, a supreme showman, with flair and flamboyance, was a gambler not only on cards and horses but on people too, and his success in the human field could be measured by the vast crowds who assembled along the six-mile route of his funeral from the *Daily Express* building in Great Ancoats Street, Manchester, to the cemetery.

'They called him provocative because he raised so many eyebrows by his writings – many even believed he went out of his way deliberately to cause commotion – but the truth of the matter is that Henry wrote what he believed to be correct, and, right or wrong, provoked heated discussion out of the forthright nature of his approach.

'They called him an egotist, and probably with some justification, but he was also a sensitive man, anxious to please, never to hurt, and proud of popularity more than personal power. For that reason he was always mindful of the problems of others and ever ready to help the less fortunate.

'It used to be said of Henry that he never entered a hotel or sporting arena without making sure that others were conscious of the fact. He was even known to arrange his own paging in hotels – just to advertise his presence – and more than once he enjoyed the reaction of sporting crowds to such prearranged announcements from the comfort of the press seats, where his entrances often got more acclaim than the appearances of rival contenders.

'Such an occasion was York City's triumph over Middlesbrough on a cold blustery day before the Second World War on one of their FA Cup giant-killing runs, when the biggest single cheer from a record crowd heralded Henry's beautifully timed arrival in the Press box.

'As could only be expected of one so outspoken in his columns Henry often got himself into hot water with authority and into deeper, if more jocular, trouble with readers ever ready to pounce on any flaws in opinions and predictions noted for being more consistently bold than accurate.

'He once wrote that if Tommy Taylor, the Manchester United centre forward, was worthy of his England place, then he himself was Father Christmas, but with typical humility he was apologizing soon afterwards after seeing Taylor in a starring role.

'They died together in friendship.'

Eric Todd, of *The Guardian*, knew H.D. (Donny) Davies as 'Jack and master of all trades' and said: 'He was a man of divers talents which he used for the profit and above all the pleasure of mankind the world over.

'He was a happy little man – like Mrs Fezziwig, "one vast substantial smile" – and in his cloth cap and plus-fours, invariably carrying his personal rug in all weathers, he would arrive early at a football match not so much to make sure of getting a seat as to exchange greetings with all who passed through the main entrance. A private welcoming committee no less.

'For most of his working life, Davies was an education

officer with a Manchester engineering firm. When it was suggested that he took up "serious" writing, he offered his part-time services to the then *Manchester Guardian.* And was turned down. Whereupon he sent to the editor an imaginary report of a football match and was engaged forthwith.

'He was an essayist rather than a reporter and in the words of Neville Cardus he "made full use of digression". Not that he ever sought refuge in "quotes" in order to fill up his space, but he would enlarge on some incident which nobody but he had seen and, if necessary, interpolate irrelevant references to mankind in general. Yet he made every word count to one end or another. Monday morning breakfast was made the more satisfying by a football report by "Old International".

'He created an interest in the game in the most improbable places, and people who knew little about the game and cared even less read him for sheer enjoyment.

'"Old International" was no misleading pseudonym. Don Davies, a Northern Nomad, played for England amateurs against Wales in 1914 – Ivan Sharpe, another great literator, was in the same side. He also had a season with Lancashire county cricket team and in between times he played bowls with enthusiasm. In fact he did most things and did them well.

'For all his literary talents and qualities as an after-dinner speaker, I imagine that Davies will be remembered best for his broadcasting. Tom Cragg, long forgotten by most people, was a master of the spoken word on sound radio before the war, and Don Davies was a worthy successor. There never has been anyone to compare remotely with either of them in their capacity for mixing uncomplicated commonsense with a generous flavouring of instinctive humour. Both were men of and for the people, and there was nothing phoney in their make-ups.

'It was ironical that Don Davies should lose his life in an aeroplane crash some forty years after he had been shot down and taken prisoner while serving with the Royal Flying

Corps. When he was released, he was given six months to live. Providence and Don Davies himself decided otherwise.'

Peter Thomas, associate editor of the *Daily Express* and a former northern sports editor of the *Daily Mirror*, remembered Eric Thompson (*Daily Mail*), George Follows (*Daily Herald*) and Archie Ledbrooke (*Daily Mirror*) for different reasons.

'Eric Thompson was the smile on the face of gentleness,' said Peter. 'To him journalism was not a weapon but a thing of joy, happiness. His life was a chuckle.

'Times were not always kind to Eric; he rode a lusty stallion to fame, but always managed to keep his seat, and when he dismounted for a rest would rub his backside with a gentle smile.

'He was the J. B. Priestley of Manchester journalism, avuncular, knowing, wise, and his humour was broader than J.B.'s and not as acrid. There were many funny things he said, with just a pucker at the corner of his mouth. When you passed them on, you only felt a deep shame that you had tried to emulate the master. He once said . . . but there I go. Why should I tell you now what Eric decided not to print under his own name?

'He should have been a professional press-box entertainer, forever making sad men smile, making the obvious remark unobviously, and teaching you that a game is just a game for a' that.

'George Follows was perhaps the best writer. I knew two Georges. George the first, the younger, and George the second, the matured writer of wit and cut.

'As young men eager to make stars and moonbeams out of the Third Division (North), we travelled often together, both of us peering through steel-rimmed services glasses, and George the first writing like a Cardus on the Trinidad Steel Band.

'George the second wrote easily, but now he became refined, always particular to rise above his subject, which always seemed to be soccer, glancing now from behind majestically horn-rimmed glasses and licking his lips in great satisfaction as Eddie Colman triumphed.

'Archie Ledbrooke was a man who almost beat the Munich disaster. It was the journalistic drive that drove him to his death. Archie was tall, bald, authoritative; he believed in managers, directors and Fred Howarth, then the League secretary.

'He believed most of all in Joe Smith, the Blackpool manager, for whom he had a love and affection which he did not accord to many.

'The night before the plane took off for Belgrade, Archie had to finish a three-part piece on Joe Smith for the *Daily Mirror*. He hadn't finished it. Unfortunately, I was the person who had to give him the ultimatum that either he finished it that night or Frank McGhee took the trip instead.

'At nine o'clock on the night before the flight, Archie finished the three-part series. Archie went with Manchester United and Archie died.

'He was a donnish sort of journalist; aloof, remote, yet at the same time the sort of person a young journalist could turn to for advice. He might not always get it, but he would get one hell of a good answer. He was remote and friendly; he was formidable and approachable and his great love was Lancashire cricket. It seemed to me ironic that he should die flying with a football team.'

Two of the reporters played each other in a journalistic 'Derby' game every day. Eric Cooper remembered them well and said: 'You could say that Alf Clarke and Tom Jackson lived *and* died together, because after some twenty-five years of friendly rivalry they were probably identified as much by their love of Manchester United, coupled with "Casual Comments" and "United Topics" in the club programme, as for their much greater journalistic activities on the same subject, Alf with the *Manchester Evening Chronicle* and Tom the *Manchester Evening News*.

160

'Yet in all other things they were entirely different characters.

'Slim-line Alf, built for the role as one of the smartest dressers in sporting journalism, was almost religious in his possessive pride for United, but carried his fervour with a serious-minded quiet and caution that suggested he was ever mindful of less successful times before the war.

'Tom was a rounder figure, a "comfortable" chap, with a ready smile and a happy greeting, and if United's post-war rise added to his labours, the successes were also more attuned to his image.

'Pages could no doubt be written about Tom's constant war with his inseparable "enemy", chasing telephone calls, club gossip and team news – the kind of things that beset all sports journalists but here magnified by the importance of the United topic in a successful soccer city.

'But it is no detriment to his journalistic ability that when work was done Tom could easily have been mistaken for just one more happy official in a highly successful football club. Such was his keenness, his loyalty and his warmth of character.'

Said Eric Todd: 'There are many pitfalls and temptations for a writer whose working life is spent covering the activities of one team, especially when that team is Manchester United. Alf, like Tom, was a great and popular character, and although both were unrepentant chauvinists, they wrote what they honestly believed their readers wanted to read.

'As Alf used to say, "There's only one team in this city and you can't write enough about them". Alf and Tom had readers in abundance and that was the object of their exercise. When you are not read and not criticized, then is the time to start worrying.

'For widely different reasons, Sir Matt Busby and Alf Clarke were the best publicity officers Manchester United ever had. Matt, of course, was the more accomplished player – nobody ever imagined Alf as a manager – but Alf was on

United's books as an amateur long before Matt arrived on the scene.

'If he had not adopted journalism as a career and if there had been no Manchester United, Alf might well have made a name for himself in the world of music – he was a brilliant pianist and boy chorister at Manchester Cathedral – and snooker, a game at which he was a local amateur champion.

'Some people accused Alf of being biased, but that was an understatement. Whenever United were defeated, Alf always had an excuse for them, usually that "the ball ran unkindly".

'I remember Hull City winning 2–0 in an FA Cup tie in 1952 at Old Trafford. On the following Monday morning when Alf walked into the Withy Grove offices, everyone in the editorial department stood with heads bowed as a token of respect for the departed United. Alf sat down at his desk completely oblivious of the "mourners" and typed his piece explaining how Fortune so cruelly had turned her back on his loved ones.

'Alf had established phrases for every set of circumstances. When the draw was made for any round of the FA Challenge Cup, as soon as he knew whom United would meet – be the opposition Arsenal or Rochdale – Alf's answer to inquiries about United's chances was always, "They'll declare at half time".

'He did not always see eye to eye with the England selectors and of certain players who were rated highly elsewhere, Alf's most telling comment was, "They wouldn't get in United's 'A' team".

'Alf endured agony in the summer because it meant no United and he had to report on Lancashire cricket. He enjoyed playing rather than watching – he once made a century on a local park – and alway insisted that Lancashire's headquarters was a "waste of a bloody good ground".

'I imagine that if he had had his way, Manchester United would have occupied both Old Traffords, one for matches and the other for training purposes. When I took over Alf's cricket reporting duties in 1947, his relief and gratitude were very obvious.

'If they talk about football in the Elysian fields – and there is no evidence to the contrary – Alf Clarke will not permit anyone to denigrate Manchester United. And I wouldn't mind wagering a modest sum that already he has convinced many among the unseen host that United will be back in the First Division next year.'

Frank Swift was representing the *News of the World*, but the world knew 'Big Swifty' as one of the greatest goalkeepers of all time, a former Manchester City team-mate of Matt Busby, who paid this tribute in his book *Soccer at the Top*:

'Big Swifty was one of the greatest and certainly the most cheerful character I have come across in a game which, in the grim, unsmiling days of the seventies, could do with a few like him.

'Swifty was a mere boy when he played with me in City's winning Cup Final against Portsmouth in 1934. The occasion proved too much for him and at the end of it he fainted. Trying to pull himself together in the dressing room afterwards he stammered: "Have we won?"

'Many years later, talking to a friend of mine, Frank told of the time when he was very young, playing for City against Birmingham. Alec Herd took a free kick from thirty yards out and the ball was in the net before the great Harry Hibbs could move. At the end of the game, as they went off together, the boy Swift said to the master Hibbs: "What happened with Alec's free kick?" – and the great man said: "If you can't see 'em, son, you can't stop 'em."

'Big Swifty fainted only once in a dressing room. He developed into the cheeriest dressing-room man in the game of football, whether playing for Manchester City or England. In any company he was a brilliant raconteur. In the dressing room his infectious good humour brought a smile to even the most nervous beginner.

'On the pitch he was the first showman goalkeeper. But

before all he was a magnificent goalkeeper, secondly a showman. He believed in entertaining the crowd. He played with a smile and with banter to match. Some opponent would send in a mighty shot. The big hands of Big Swifty would envelop it as if it had been a gentle lob. "Good shot, that, Joe," he would say to the man who had cracked it in.

'No matter who was captain there was only one boss in Swifty's goal. It went without saying, though he said it often enough: "If I shout, get out of my way. If you don't, I'll knock you out of the way." He was the first goalkeeper I saw who threw the ball out, accurately and over great distances, to a colleague, instead of merely punting it up the pitch and giving the other team an equal chance of getting it. He would pick it up one-handed and throw it like a cricket ball.

'For a big man, Swifty was phenomenally agile. He narrowed the angle for an opponent to shoot in as if he had made a science of it. His showmanship was not exhibitionism. He wanted to demonstrate that football could include a bit of fun, a quality sadly missing from the game today. He was immensely popular everywhere he played, as popular with opposition and opposition supporters as with his own team and his own team's supporters. If any footballer could be termed lovable, Big Swifty was the man.

'But there was just one occasion when I wished him miles away from me. He was playing for England, I for Scotland, before about 125,000 people at Hampden Park, Glasgow. We had played together for Manchester City for years. We knew each other's play with a familiarity born of hours and years of practice together and many, many matches together. We Scots had discussed who should take penalty kicks, and though I did not want to take them we decided I should do so.

'At the height of interest in the match, when England were leading 3–1 but Scotland were well on top and striving desperately to reduce the lead, we were awarded a penalty. My problem was Frank Swift. I had taken a thousand penalty kicks against him at practice. He knew my style. He knew where I liked to place them and where I almost always tried to place them.

'It seems impossible as I set this down that all the thoughts that went through my mind did so as I took the short walk to place the ball, the few steps back, and the run-up to kick it. Shall I place the ball to Frank's left, since he will be expecting it to go, as usual, to his right? On the other hand, I cogitated, he might well say to himself: "I know Matt, he will try to kid me by putting it to my left side, so I will dive left."

'But then, I thought, Frank will guess that I have seen through his reasoning and he will see through mine and he will dive to his right. Anyway, I put it to his right.

'Frank dived, and saved it.

'There was a groan from 100,000 Scottish throats, a cheer from 25,000 English ones, then a great low, grumbling noise as of people telling their fellows where one player ought to go and that player was Matt Busby. At Hampden Park that day I wished Frank Swift, my old pal, was far away.

'I was with Big Swifty from his beginnings in League football. And I was with him when he died at Munich. He was only forty-three. He died when he had much fun still in him to share with friends, neighbours and strangers.'

Mike Dempsey, now northern sports editor of the *Daily Express*, recalled the days of farewell to the men he had so admired:

'The mornings and afternoons seemed to be an endless procession of cortèges, flowers, tears and memories. Black ties must have been worn out at the end,' he said.

'The biggest funeral of all was Henry Rose's, the most read sporting journalist the *Daily Express* ever had, or will ever have, because that breed has gone now.

'Manchester's thousand-strong taxi fleet volunteered transport free for anyone who wanted to be at the funeral. The *Express* office was bulging with staff from three centres.

'A vivid memory; everyone had to wear hats for the Jewish

service. I have never seen such a collection. Homburgs, bowlers, caps, trilbies, berets, headscarves, anything so long as people could join the six-mile queue to Southern Cemetery.

'They stopped Henry's hearse outside the office. We all filed into the taxis that had no meters running. I was in a taxi that, by the time it had passed the "enemy" camp at Maine Road, the leading cars were already treble-parked at the cemetery. I never even got inside the gates.

'Back in the office I witnessed another master of words perform the greatest single piece of work I have ever seen. Desmond Hackett – another hero of mine – walked in, doffed his famous brown bowler, took off his jacket, sat there in his red braces and within twenty minutes had written something like seven hundred words that began, "Even the skies wept for Henry Rose today . . .". A magnificent epitaph for a really remarkable man.

'Most of those I knew were the journalists. I had the privilege of doing the soccer circuit with them all. And just as Munich will never turn up a team to match the one that died so too journalism will never ever find a group of sports journalists like those who died with that team.

'Munich not only changed the face of Manchester United's football; it changed the face of sporting journalism. The deaths of so many men of stature began the era of "bought" stories, cheque-book sports pages, and virtually ended the scoop a week that these men practised, got away with and survived even if they didn't.

'These men matched the team they all loved in stature and skill. I don't think there will ever be another team that had such heights of perfection, yet such unassuming airs about the whole game. They just loved playing.

'After the crash I recall the first match at Old Trafford. A night of incredible emotion. Weeping, wailing, and even fans shouting inadvertently the names of dead players when the excitement overtook them. The waves of emotion lasted for the whole of that season and beyond.

'I don't think Manchester has been the same since. Not even the triumphs since can obscure the memories of a team that I am convinced would have swept the world trophies for at least another six years. People who never saw them haven't really seen the absolute in football. I could never hope to see that same again.'

14. The Aftermath

James Patrick Murphy, a Celt if ever there was one, born in the Rhondda of a Welsh mother and Irish father, poured a lifetime of heartbreak and mental and physical torment into the crowded weeks that followed the disaster. He saved United, pulled together the flimsy fabric of what was left of a great club and somehow kept his sanity, commonsense and judgement to be able to ride the waves of emotion that washed over Manchester.

Thinking back to that incredible time, he described the team's recovery as 'A miracle. Nothing to do with Jimmy Murphy, all due to our good Lord.'

Murphy, the Welsh international team manager, had stayed behind to guide his country successfully through a World Cup qualifying match against Israel in Cardiff.

'I usually sat next to Matt on the plane and had the next room to his at the hotel whenever the team went away and I had suggested that I went to Belgrade, with it being such an important European Cup game. He had said, "No, Jimmy, you have a job to do", so Bert Whalley went to Belgrade in my place,' he recalled.

'I will never forget that Thursday. I arrived back in Manchester by train from Cardiff and had with me a large box of oranges presented to me by the Israelis. I got a taxi, put the box of oranges inside, and off we went to Old Trafford.

'Usually there was a lot of activity at the ground, but when I arrived everything seemed very quiet. I lifted out the box of oranges, put it inside the main entrance and went upstairs to the boardroom, carrying my briefcase.

'It had been a long, tiring journey and I poured myself a glass of Scotch. Alma George, Matt's secretary, came in and told me about the crash. I didn't take it in at all. I just poured Alma a glass of sherry and carried on sipping my Scotch.

'"I don't think you understand," said Alma. "The plane has crashed. A lot of people have died." She was right. I did not understand. So she told me a third time, and this time she started to cry. A good few minutes had elapsed and suddenly Alma's words began to take effect on me. I went into my office and cried.

'Suddenly, after all the silence, the ground came to life again as the telephones began a ceaseless ringing and relatives started to arrive. It is hard to describe how difficult things became. That night as I answered the telephones and tried to sort out just what had happened, I went through a bottle of Scotch without even noticing it.

'Next day I flew to Munich with the relatives of the survivors and saw firsthand the suffering and the heartbreak. I saw Duncan Edwards, who mumbled, "Oh, it's you, Jimmy. Is the kick-off three o'clock?" He was still thinking of the next match even though he was so terribly injured. And Matt was in an oxygen tent and, as I bent close, he whispered, "Keep the flag flying, Jimmy".

'Matt had not long been out of hospital before the trip to Belgrade. He had had a minor operation on his legs.

'I travelled back with Bill Foulkes and Harry Gregg and, amid all the tragedy and all the sorrow, I had to get a team together again. I had to find players from somewhere.

'How can I describe what it was like? I was completely alone, isolated. There was no Matt Busby, no Bert Whalley. No one I could talk with on my level as far as the team was concerned.

'People wanted to help but they could not give me the help I wanted. I didn't need people to open letters and help in ways like that. I needed players. Liverpool and Nottingham Forest offered to do what they could, but I was left trying to sort out what I had, what I needed and what I could get. And the relatives kept coming to the ground, naturally, anxious for the latest news.

'Then the coffins started to arrive at the ground. We put them in the old gymnasium, which was where the players' lounge is now. And there were all the funerals. And all the time I was wondering where I could get players. The game against Wolves had been postponed, but things had to be done quickly. No one knows what I went through during that time.

'I managed to sign Ernie Taylor from Blackpool and he did a magnificent job for us with his skill and experience. He had been offered a job by Sunderland, but Paddy McGrath, our friend from the Cromford Club, brought Ernie over to see me and I managed to persuade him to join us over a glass of beer.

'It was important to get the players away from Old Trafford, away from the atmosphere of death, away from Manchester and all the emotion. We virtually lived at the Norbreck Hydro in Blackpool.'

Bill Foulkes remembered those days vividly: 'We had to get away from Manchester,' he said. 'Everyone meant well, of course, but the last thing we needed was their sympathy. It was terribly difficult and upsetting. Ernie Taylor played a wonderful part in our fight back and it was a difficult time for him because he had just lost his son in a road accident.'

Murphy thought of signing Ferenc Puskas, who had left his native Hungary after the uprising, but reasoned that the maximum wage and restriction on foreign players would make such a move almost impossible. But he did sign Taylor for £8000 and then approached Aston Villa for hard-tackling Stan Crowther, a man who had helped to end United's FA Cup dreams the previous May.

Villa manager, Eric Houghton, put the proposition to Crowther, who said he did not want to leave Villa. Houghton then asked Crowther if he would go with him to watch United play their FA Cup tie against Sheffield Wednesday, thirteen days after Munich, and Crowther agreed.

To help United, the Football Association had allowed United to rearrange that fifth round tie and had also waived the rule which prevented a player from representing more than one club in the FA Cup in any one season.

On the way to the match, Houghton told Crowther: 'You ought to help them.' Crowther said he had not got his boots. 'I've brought them with me,' said Houghton.

They met Murphy at United's hotel and Crowther was persuaded to sign for a fee of £22,000 less than an hour before he played in the match.

It was an experience Manchester will never forget as a crowd of 60,000 poured into Old Trafford. The poignancy of the occasion was symbolized by the match programme, in which the team sheet contained eleven blank spaces where the names of the United players should have been.

Murphy made Foulkes captain to lead out a team including two survivors (Foulkes and Gregg), five reserves who had made rare first team appearances and youngsters Mark Pearson and Shay Brennan, who were making their debuts, and new signings Taylor and Crowther.

Sheffield were beaten by the emotion before they had a chance to kick the ball. United won 3–0 and Brennan, usually a wing half, scored two of the goals.

'I played Shay Brennan on the left wing and he scored one of those goals straight from a corner kick,' said Murphy. 'It was amazing how we made progress with a mixture of the players I signed and lads from the reserves and "A" team. But what we did have above all else was the interests of the club at heart.'

In the sixth round, United were drawn away to West Bromwich Albion, who were in the middle of a fine run of form and had beaten Arsenal 5–1 in the third round.

But United, with Ernie Taylor inspiring them from mid-field, led 2–1 with four minutes to play. Then Gregg caught the ball on his goal line, the referee ruled he had carried it over, and Albion won a replay.

Bobby Charlton had been fit enough to rejoin the team, and 60,000 fanatics willed United to win the replay. But Albion attacked from the start and were finishing the stronger side when, with barely a minute to play, Ronnie Cope ended a dangerous Albion attack and swept the ball upfield to Charlton. Charlton beat three defenders and crossed the ball to the far post, where Colin Webster scored the only goal. United were in the semi-finals.

United met Fulham at Villa Park, and Charlton took a pass from Taylor to shoot them ahead after twelve minutes with a volley from the edge of the penalty box.

Arthur Stevens equalized for Fulham, and Jimmy (the Beard) Hill put them ahead with a powerful shot. Fulham left back Jim Langley was injured and had to leave the field for treatment. While he was off, Charlton scored again with a wonderful shot after one from Mark Pearson had been blocked. It was 2–2 at half time, and stayed that way even though Charlton went close again, with Fulham goalkeeper Tony Macedo getting a finger tip to the ball.

The nation watched the replay on television – coverage was advertised the day before – and the attendance of 38,258 at Highbury was lower than anticipated. United brought in Brennan for Pearson at outside left, and attacked Fulham from the start.

It was not a happy game for goalkeeper Macedo. He missed the ball to give centre forward Alex Dawson the chance to head United's first goal in the thirteenth minute. Stevens equalized, but Macedo made another slip and a shot from Dawson passed under his body to put United 2–1 up.

'Tosh' Chamberlain equalized for Fulham three minutes later following a brilliant run by Langley, but Macedo failed to anticipate a back pass a minute from the interval, and Brennan gave United a 3–2 lead. Dawson completed his hat-trick nineteen minutes after half time, and though Roy Dwight pulled Fulham back to 4–3 with fifteen minutes to play, Charlton scored a fifth goal for United in the last minute.

United were back at Wembley, where they made one change for the final against Bolton Wanderers. Dennis Viollet had played one game since the crash but was judged to be ready. Matt Busby managed to make the trip to London to watch the final.

It was the day everyone at Wembley sang the hymn 'Abide With Me' with great feeling before the teams emerged from the dressing rooms, United wearing special crests on the left breasts of their shirts, the emblem of the phoenix rising from the ashes. But for the millions who willed United to win the Final, it was to be an anti-climax.

Nat Lofthouse, played onside by Crowther when the other United defenders had moved forward following a speculative shot by Bryan Edwards, gave Bolton an early lead.

A shot from Charlton hit a post, but Bolton scored a second goal when Doug Holden crossed high – and Lofthouse charged Gregg as he came out to gain possession, then knocked the ball over the line. For the second successive year, United's final challenge was unhinged by a charge on their goalkeeper; McParland on Wood in '57, Lofthouse on Gregg in '58.

'When we lost to Bolton it was worse than ever,' recalled Foulkes. 'I'll never forget our arrival back in Manchester. Millions of people seemed to be there to meet us.

'I couldn't see a chink of light because of the crowds at the station, and it was the same all the way to Albert Square.

'The Square was jammed, and so were the streets leading from it. People were crying. Even when we were inside the Town Hall they kept shouting for us. But I couldn't go out. I just couldn't face it that time. I broke down.'

Busby was back, but still a long way from fitness. 'I was still on sticks when I went to Wembley and, though I was proud of what Jimmy Murphy and the boys had achieved in getting to the Final, I was also very sad,' he said.

'I was still not well, physically and mentally, and the occasion upset me emotionally. I was not able to go down to see the team after the game. I did not feel up to it. I had to go away. I think I just wanted to sleep.

'After that I went away for a rest. I went to Interlaken for about six weeks and that was just what I needed. That made me live again.

'It must have been a terrible time for Jimmy and everyone at the club after the crash, with so much sadness and emotion. It needed someone who, though feeling the heartbreak of the situation, could still keep his head and keep the job going. Jimmy was that man and he did a wonderful job of holding the fort.'

Five days after their defeat at Wembley, United beat A.C. Milan 2–1 in the first leg of the European Cup semi-final, but lost the return game 4–0 in Italy. Bobby Charlton missed both games because of England international duty. But at the time there can be no doubt that United's need of Charlton was the greater.

The brief but glorious era of 'The Babes' had ended, but the efforts of Murphy and his patchwork team had assured United of a future; perhaps never quite approaching the breathtaking potential of the immediate past ... but when would another club team ever manage that?

What began to emerge was the third great team built by Busby and Murphy, for the spirit of 1958 was not allowed to die.

'The following season we finished as runner-up to Wolves in the championship and that was remarkable because we were not really equipped to do so well so soon,' recalled Busby.

'Looking back, there was, I suppose, a period of five or six years when events dictated our policy. There had been a break in the continuity of our planning and we had to stretch our playing resources beyond the limits.

'Young players with tremendous potential whom we planned to work on and groom over a period of years – boys like Mark Pearson, Alex Dawson and so many others – had to be thrust forward ahead of time.

'We had no alternative, but this obviously took its toll. There was no breathing space, no let up, and to keep the job ticking over we had to go out and buy players we needed.

'For a while, perhaps, we had to neglect the youth policy. The important thing was to keep our name to the fore-front and to help achieve this we brought over Real Madrid. We were determined to piece together again as soon as possible.'

Busby and Murphy were far too busy rebuilding and planning at the time to indulge themselves in their achievements since the end of the war.

Tom Finney, the Preston and England winger whose ability is reflected in the fact that he was twice voted Footballer of the Year (1954 and 1957) during the period of The Babes, called United 'The Arsenal of the North'.

Finney regards Busby's 1948 FA Cup-winning side as *the* team, but says: 'By the same token we had not by any means seen the best of The Babes. It would have been intriguing . . .'

A glance at the following statistics from 1952–3 to 1958–9 will underline the greatness and the potential lost at Munich.

LEAGUE									FA CUP
P	W	L	D	F	A	Pts	Pstn		
42	18	14	10	69	72	46	8	1952–3	5th round
42	18	12	12	73	54	48	4	1953–4	3rd round
42	20	15	7	84	74	47	5	1954–5	4th round
42	25	7	10	83	51	60	1	1955–6	3rd round
42	28	6	8	103	54	64	1	1956–7	Final tie
42	16	15	11	85	75	43	9	1957–8	Final tie
42	24	11	7	103	66	55	2	1958–9	3rd round

Stan Pearson	15	1952–3	Allenby Chilton
Tommy Taylor	22	1953–4	Allenby Chilton
Tommy Taylor	20	1954–5	————
Dennis Viollet	20		
Tommy Taylor	25	1955–6	Mark Jones
Liam Whelan	26	1956–7	————
Dennis Viollet	17	1957–8	Bill Foulkes
Bobby Charlton	29	1958–9	Freddie Goodwin
			Albert Scanlon

EUROPEAN CUP

In season 1956–7 United lost to Real Madrid (1–3 away, 2–2 at home) after defeating Anderlecht, Borussia Dortmund, and Atletico Bilbao.

In season 1957–8 United lost to A.C. Milan (2–1 at home, 0–4 away) after defeating Shamrock Rovers, Dukla (Prague), and Red Star (Belgrade).

Before United could become a force again, an important psychological barrier had to be overcome, as Foulkes recalled: 'About a year after the crash, the boss arranged a friendly game against Feyenoord in Rotterdam. He said we would have to get used to flying again if we were to continue playing in Europe and he thought it was a good idea to start with a short trip.

'I suppose we all worried in our own ways, but the flight went well. When I arrived in my hotel room in Rotterdam, I put a telephone call through to my wife, but Teresa said she had already heard we had landed safely.

'The boss had stayed behind at the airport and phoned Old Trafford to make sure our wives were told everything had gone smoothly.'

United's loss began to be reflected more clearly when the club had to go into the transfer market for new players. Whereas the 1948 team had cost £7750 (Carey £250, Rowley £3500 and Delaney £4000) and Busby had spent £84,999 on the 1958 team (Wood £6000, Gregg £24,000, Berry £25,000 and Taylor £29,999) the next period was punctuated with the following cheques: Albert Quixall (£45,000), Maurice Setters (£30,000), Noel Cantwell (£29,000), David Herd (£40,000), Denis Law (£115,000), Pat Crerand (£43,000), Graham Moore (£35,000), John Connelly (£56,250) and Alex Stepney (£52,000); a total outlay of £445,250.

But behind this spending, boys were still being spotted and nurtured through the juniors. Boys like Nobby Stiles, who used to clean the boots of the great players who died at Munich and who afterwards asked if he could keep the pair that belonged to Tommy Taylor. The request was granted.

'We had another great crop of youngsters at the start of the 1960s when we won the FA Youth Cup again,' emphasized Busby. 'Boys started to come through like John Fitzpatrick, Bobby Noble, Willie Anderson, John Aston and, of course, George Best. And there was Francis Burns and Brian Kidd. Boys were still keen to join Manchester United.

'We did start to rebuild again on the old, familiar, successful lines, though not all youngsters with potential come right through to the first team, and some are not fortunate enough to avoid serious injury. We have had our successes and also our disappointments in this respect.'

Bill Foulkes lost his place and asked to be relieved of his captaincy, but he was at centre half in the team Noel Cantwell led to a 3–1 victory over Leicester City to win the FA Cup in 1963 ... a year in which United had come perilously close to relegation.

Johnny Giles, a star of the Cup success even though he had been unsettled at Old Trafford following the FA Cup semi-final the previous season, when United were beaten 3–1 by Tottenham Hotspur, was dropped from the first team to make way for Ian Moir early in the 1963–4 season and he asked for a transfer.

Less than a week later, on 29 August 1963, Giles was sold to Leeds United for £37,000, and played a vital role in Don Revie's success story.

Even so, United's resurgence was gaining momentum as Stiles and Best came through to add their extra special talents to those of the established first teamers.

United won the League Championship in 1965 on goal average from Leeds, and again in 1967, four points ahead of Nottingham Forest and unbeaten at home. In between was another European Cup semi-final, with United losing 2–1 on aggregate to Partizan, of Belgrade, but building surely towards a grand climax.

In 1968, ten years after Munich, Foulkes played a major role in bringing the European Cup to Old Trafford. United, appropriately, met Real Madrid in the semi-final and travelled to Madrid with a 1–0 lead from the first leg. But by half time, Madrid were leading 3–1 in the return game.

'We felt a bit sick in the dressing room at half time,' said Foulkes, 'and I knew this was my last chance in the competition. But they were outplaying us. I don't think we had a great team then by former standards and we were far from our best in that first half.

'But Matt made the point that it was only 3–2 really, on aggregate, and we only needed a goal to force a replay in Lisbon, because there would be no extra time.

'So we went out and found that instead of coming at us and pressurizing us, Madrid started playing the ball about, believing they had done enough and only had to contain us.

'That gave us more chance to attack and David Sadler put the ball in off a knee. That meant we were level on aggregate, and gave us tremendous heart.

'We won a throw in and Paddy Crerand had the ball on the touchline. The game was delicately balanced, and Paddy was determined not to waste a ball. He was looking for men to move forward to create possibilities. He must have made about half a dozen attempts to throw without being helped by a man moving into the right position.

'I started to jog upfield and eventually called out to Paddy. As he made as if to throw the ball to me he saw that the full back who had done such a good job marking George Best had moved slightly. Paddy turned and sent George away, and I just kept jogging upfield.

'George took his man on, beat him and was moving towards the line and shaping to cross the ball. I could see that their defence had the near post well covered so that a conventional cross would have been cut out. Fortunately, George saw it, too, and cut the ball back to where I was.

'I won't say I shot the ball, but as it came across I could see the target clearly, about two-thirds of the goal. I sort of passed the ball in the direction of the target, striking it firmly with the inside of my right boot. It went into the net beautifully – the best sidefoot pass I ever made!

'I took less than two steps and was surrounded by team-mates with their congratulations, but I said, "Let's get the game finished". There were about twenty minutes left, but we held Madrid comfortably. They attacked again but were up against a different team. Every one of us was playing well now. There was no way they could keep us from the final.

'And once we had reached that final, at Wembley, I had no doubts about us winning, even when it was 1–1 at the end of normal time, after we had taken the lead with a Bobby Charlton header. Eusebio had broken clear with a great chance to win the game right near the end of ninety minutes. Alex Stepney seemed to move out of his goal too quickly, but Eusebio struck the ball hastily and Alex got right behind the ball, and it stuck.

'I knew we were going to win then, and we murdered Benfica in extra time to beat them 4–1.' United's goals were scored by Charlton (2), Best and Kidd.

Foulkes thought for a moment before adding: 'I should have packed in then. I had achieved everything I could as a player and the nastiness of the World Club Championship game against Estudiantes in Argentina the following year really sickened me.'

Triumph in Europe marked the end of two glorious

decades at Old Trafford. United's decline was first gradual and then dramatic, and in 1974, the club was relegated to the Second Division for the first time for thirty-six years.

The men who had been a part of the most remarkable days for United when greatness was young and tomorrow never came had enjoyed varying fortunes. Some were established as managers in League football, like Freddie Goodwin, who had served his apprenticeship at Scunthorpe United and in the United States and, in 1974, had indirectly played a role in the downfall of Old Trafford as the manager of Birmingham City who had saved themselves from relegation partly at United's expense.

Ray Wood, injury victim of the 1957 Cup Final, was director of coaching in Kuwait, having found his way to that unlikely outpost by way of Huddersfield Town, where he was a player, Canada, Bradford City and Barnsley, where he was a player-coach, Los Angeles Wolves, in the United States, Zambia, Dublin, Cork and Cyprus, where he had been national team manager and coach. Ernie Taylor finally left football and became a shop steward in the motor car industry, working at Vauxhall Motors, Ellesmere Port, Cheshire.

Bill Foulkes, armed with coaching certificates, a diploma from a managerial course and the experience of a million situations with great teams, left Old Trafford, where he had coached the reserve team, and pursued an ambition to prove himself in the hard, lonely world of club management. He became manager of Witney Town, in the Southern League, and had thoughts about a job in American soccer.

Foulkes had seen it all.

'I don't mind talking about the crash now,' he said. 'But it was quite some time before I could face things again.

'At first I could not bear to go to Davyhulme Golf Club because of all the memories. The players always gathered there before matches and we used to play cards and relax before going on to Old Trafford in the team coach.

'I didn't play golf in those days. I couldn't see any sense in knocking a little white ball around a course, though later the game took a hold of me.'

The bookshelves of his home at Sale, Cheshire, were filled with volumes about the golfing greats.

'I think the crash affected us all in some way. Before it happened, Bobby Charlton was a quiet, confident lad. Afterwards I noticed that he seemed more nervous. His hand used to shake a little when he held a cup and saucer, and I noticed traces of the same thing when he used to smoke.

'Some of the lads, like Johnny Berry and Jackie Blanchflower, never played again. Others played, but were never as effective. Before the crash, I was the type who would save every penny. Afterwards, I began to live for the moment and spend money as if it was going out of fashion. I lost a hell of a lot of weight, too.

'Teresa and I decided to have a family, and Stephen, the eldest of our three children, was born within a year.

'I've talked about the crash to Harry Gregg, because we were involved together. But I've never talked about it to Dennis Viollet, not even when he was over from America, where he is in charge of a soccer club in Washington. And I've never mentioned it to Bobby Charlton or to Matt.

'It's just something that never crops up. Something there is no need to discuss amongst ourselves, because we know only too well all there is to know about it.'

Bobby Charlton is a rare blessing in the narration of this story, for he is the link between past and present, breaching all argument as living proof of how great were 'The Babes'.

He was the cannonball kid from the reserves who had just begun to make the grade pre-Munich, and his career, bejewelled with honours and an untarnished reputation, is a fair guideline to the potential of the team as a whole.

Charlton went on to complete 606 League games for United, scoring 199 goals, and won an FA Cup winner's medal in 1963, League Championship medals in 1965 and

1967, a World Cup winner's medal in 1966 and a European Cup winner's medal in 1968. In 1966 he was England's Footballer of the Year and Europe's Footballer of the Year and he made a total of 106 appearances for England, scoring 49 goals. He is now Bobby Charlton, CBE.

Having experienced the good times and the hard times at Old Trafford, he had left and spent a year as a manager – a year in which his new club, Preston, slipped into the Third Division.

Always the type to learn from experience, he was ready, at thirty-six, to push forward again, this time adding his physical presence to the cause by re-registering as a player.

As he looked back there was no doubt clouding his judgement as he said: 'The United team of the late 1950s was the best I ever played in. I know distance tends to lend enchantment, but I believe I am in a position to judge, because I am still playing.

'I played in other sides that could be brilliant on their day, but the difference was that with those sides you never knew when that day would be. With the United side of the fifties you knew it was always going to happen.

'There were so many great players and if you managed to get into the first team you had a tremendously high standard to reach before you were accepted.

'People talk about the fitness of the modern players but I reckon the players then were even fitter than they are today because football then was a physical game. Goalkeepers were fair game and defenders were harder and if you came through the tackle then you were a good player. It was a physical game, not a running game, and our training was on a voluntary basis. You were left to do your work and you knew just how fit you had to be to get into the side and last the pace.

'I can't go along with talk that the game is tougher today. I think it's cleaner than it's ever been. For me, the football in the late 1950s and early 1960s was the best it's ever been and, from a selfish football point of view, that United team could not have been lost at a worse time.

'It was a loss for United, for club football in general, and for the England team, particularly when you think of Duncan Edwards, who, all round, was the best player we had.

'Duncan was the lynch-pin of the England midfield and would have been for ten years. Suddenly, England had to find someone else, but you don't find players like Duncan Edwards.

There were other players, too, because there was such depth of talent in that United side.

'Later in my career I found there were some games I could go through without really pushing myself to the limit, but in the old days every game was an exhausting ninety minutes. There was no let-up. Everything was building up.

'The next game would be just as hard, and the next and the one after that. We were becoming better known all the time and the rewards were becoming greater.

'I doubt whether Real Madrid would have won as much as they did if that United side had survived. They beat us in the European Cup in 1957, but we learned from that, and we were still so very young.

'We were capable of reaching the final in 1958, perhaps even winning it. And if not then, it would have been very soon after. It was all like a fairy story really, starting with the ground being bombed in the war and capturing everyone's imagination when so many youngsters were put into the team. And as the club's reputation for handling young players grew, all the mothers wanted to send their sons to Old Trafford, which gave United a big advantage.

'I hear a lot of talk about pressures in the game today, but we had the same pressures then. It was just the same. We had big crowds, and everyone wanted to beat United.

'The difference after Munich was the commitment of the side. The team that played before the crash had nothing to prove. Those players knew they were great. Afterwards, we had everything to prove.

'What we achieved after the crash had a lot to do with enthusiasm, but it was all made possible by the work done previously by Joe Armstrong, Jimmy Murphy and Bert Whalley in bringing the lads through. We were able to manage only because there were so many good youngsters still available.

'They had to be thrown in at the deep end, but the point is they were there. Otherwise the recovery would not have been possible. Not the way it happened.

'We also had something else going for us, because immediately after the crash there was no glory for any team that beat us, because we were not really a side. Our opponents just could not win.

'I saw the Cup tie against Sheffield Wednesday and I felt sorry for Sheffield because as far as the crowd was concerned there was only one team out there.

'In the next round we got through in a replay against West Brom. We scored a late goal and we needed it because they were a far better side. The following Saturday they beat us 4–0, but they didn't get any credit for that.

'It was something like the tennis semi-final at Wimbledon between Stan Smith and Ken Rosewall, who had never won a final and was hoping to get through for a third attempt at it.

'The crowd was right behind Rosewall, but at one stage Smith had the match for the taking. Suddenly it seemed that Smith's will to win was not as great as his wish that Rosewall would not lose, and everything went against him.

'It was an amazing time for United, a time no one who experienced it could ever forget.'

Stan Crowther is now a foreman in a Wolverhampton factory specializing in taps and brass fittings and did not have happy memories of his time with United.

'I regretted the move,' he said. 'Too much was expected of me and I was not all that experienced. I might have looked ready at Villa, but at Villa I was playing in an experienced team.

'The fact is that I wanted to quit Villa and football altogether after we won the Cup, but I was persuaded to stay by friends,' added Crowther, who tended to be a loner even in the days when he was a successful footballer.

'When United played Bolton in the Cup Final, Dennis Viollet was not fully fit and Bobby Charlton was not at his best because it was too close to his experience at Munich. I was expected to cover up mistakes and couldn't play my normal game. But I had great respect for Jimmy Murphy, who helped me a lot.

'I played only one game for Matt Busby, a pre-season match in Germany. We were beaten and I was the only player dropped. I was never in the first team after that.'

He moved to Chelsea, and later was transferred to Brighton and, before he retired, he played in the Southern League for Rugby Town, where his manager was again Eric Houghton.

Johnny Berry never played again after Munich because of his injuries. He is now in business with his brother, Peter, in a sports shop, Berry brothers, in Farnborough.

Said Johnny: 'I stayed in Manchester for twelve months after Munich before I moved back down to Aldershot where I was born, and I watched the team while I was up there. When I came back to Aldershot my brother, Peter, had been injured playing for Ipswich, so we opened the business. We've had the shop for thirteen years now.

'The only time I've been back to Manchester was for Bobby Charlton's testimonial game. I don't watch much football now. I'm old-fashioned. I don't think football is what it used to be.

'I have played in a few kick-about matches locally, but nothing serious. If I was playing now I'd be happy because of the money players get today. But when people talk about crowds, we used to get 50,000 every week when I was playing. We didn't get big money then – the game's gone mad now. You were lucky in my day to get a benefit game that would bring you £750 – and the tax man would get about £400 of that.

'The whole complexion of the game has changed. These days it's not so much a case of winning as making sure not to lose. You couldn't afford to do that in my day.

'I have so many memories of my United days, but I suppose the big thing about it was the number of young boys in the team. And there were so many players. Of course, when someone gets a good idea, everyone latches on to it. Success brought the youngsters to United and now I suppose success will attract youngsters to Liverpool and clubs like that.

'I don't think you can really say the crash was responsible for the club being relegated in the long run because they had too much success after Munich, winning the FA Cup, League championships and the European Cup.

'What did happen was that the established players got older after United won the European Cup. I was saddened by United's relegation but not surprised by it. They were in trouble for two years before they went down and their form was not inspiring any confidence, with a good run for perhaps six weeks followed by a bad run for six weeks. Mind you, it's easy to say that when you're not involved.

'I enjoyed my football. Of course I did. I think it's the same in any job – if you have success at it, you enjoy it.'

Ian Greaves is now manager of the Bolton Wanderers team after leaving Huddersfield Town where, as manager, he had known three years of success, taking the club up to the First Division, and three years of decline, slipping down into Division Three.

'After Munich, apart from the personal thing, we were all shocked in the sense that we didn't feel it for a fortnight,' he said.

'Jimmy Murphy got us together, a depleted staff, and we were all in a kind of daze. We didn't believe it, even though we knew it had happened.

'When we beat Sheffield Wednesday it was an electrifying night, but there was no cheering going on in the dressing room afterwards. We were all sad.

'I always felt as if we were cheating somehow. Stepping into other people's shoes. I felt in a way I shouldn't have been there.

'Jimmy Murphy did a wonderful job. He always did, of course. His biggest asset was that he was a bit like Bill Shankly. He could make you feel good. He would tell you, "We're the greatest. You are the best players. If you play for us you must be the greatest."

'He jumped up and down and got your blood boiling. He bullied people and gave them a chasing if they didn't give one hundred per cent. If you didn't go into a tackle hard enough with him in training, he played hell with you. He could gee people up.

'Jimmy was not a likeable bloke when you were playing. (He had been called "Tapper" Murphy when he was a player.) He was the sort who would make you lose your temper – but he was always treated with tremendous respect.

'He was offered several top jobs, but I think he knew himself that he was happy with what he was doing at United. He was not the greatest diplomat. Matt was. He always had a magical touch with people.

'Jimmy was full of surprises. Like the time we played West Brom in the Cup after Munich. We stayed at a hotel in Droitwich and had the afternoon to pass away before the game that evening. We all went into the hotel lounge, which had a grand piano. Jimmy sat at the piano and we all laughed and shouted, "Give us a tune". Jimmy set off playing Chopin, Liszt and I don't know how many other classics. He was amazing. We thought he knew nothing but football and suddenly we had a new respect for Jimmy Murphy.

'Jimmy had a lot to offer, and after ten years coaching and managing I now realize just how much Jimmy did. If I wanted advice from anyone, he'd probably be the first person I'd go to. In fact, he did come to see me a couple of times when I was with Huddersfield.

'After Munich, Jimmy's reserves became the first teamers. He'd been in charge of the reserve team for two or three years, so they were his lads. He signed Stan Crowther and Ernie Taylor and the team did incredible things, because it wasn't a good side. But when Bobby Charlton and Dennis Viollet came back, things began to settle again.'

Greaves left Old Trafford in December 1959 and spent six months in the Second Division with Lincoln City. But his playing career was waning and he had two operations on an arthritic knee.

He spent two years at Oldham, and then coached non-League club Altrincham before starting his six-year spell in charge of Huddersfield.

Dennis Viollet is player-coach to Washington Diplomats in the United States and, holidays apart, is preparing to settle in America with his wife, Helen.

Viollet, who had been transferred from United to Stoke City and was later a coach at Crewe Alexandra, recalled: 'What I remember most about the pre-Munich United team was the great team spirit we had and the great times we had together off the field. We were more like brothers than pals.

'We all stuck together. I can remember Roger Byrne fighting my battles for me when I was a kid in the "A" team at sixteen. There were still a few of the old professionals playing in the Manchester League then, but if anybody tried anything with me Roger would step in and protect me.

'After Munich, other players were bought, but it was never the same again. I don't really go one hundred per cent with the theory that United's relegation in 1974 was a direct result of the Munich disaster, but I agree this is part of the reason.

'In the days when we all went to United as kids we didn't get a penny. We wanted to join the club. Matt Busby's youth policy was a success because of the number of lads who were keen to go to Old Trafford.

'Later, competition became fiercer. More and more clubs were trying to sign kids from school and some were prepared to pay up to £5000 to get a youngster. That kind of money could obviously make a difference when a lad was making up his mind.'

Harry Gregg, who was transferred to Stoke City and had later guided centre half Jim Holton when manager at Shrewsbury, left Swansea to become manager of Crewe.

'A lot of credit must go to Jimmy Murphy,' he said. 'A certain amount of our success immediately after Munich came from sentiment. No one could say we had the best part of even a decent side left. Sentiment and human emotion played a tremendous part.

'We went back to Wembley on a wave of emotion. It is hard to believe that the crash happened. It is even more difficult to believe that whatever was still there went on to Wembley again after the crash.

'But as soon as I stepped on to the pitch at Wembley it was the biggest anti-climax of all. It never happened to me on a big occasion prior to that one or since that one. But that day, and the week preceding it, there was just nothing left. It was just a flat period. When I walked out at Wembley that day I felt no tension, and you need that to be really keyed up for a big event.

'I've been to hell and back at Munich, and I suffered worse things a year after Munich when I lost my wife. I am now married again.

'People talk about the World Cup teams of 1974, but put Duncan Edwards into any of those teams and they would have been better. The Manchester United side of 1956, 1957 and 1958 was the last great side in this country, and I don't use the word "great" lightly.

'Typical of one of our team talks from Jimmy Murphy in those days was: "We attack together and we defend together".

'It was a loss for England as well as club football in England. Duncan Edwards, Tommy Taylor, Roger Byrne, David Pegg were England players, Eddie Colman was a certainty to become one and lads like Mark Jones were on the fringe.

'You don't build a club overnight, or easily find the men we had looking after us. Bert Whalley and Tom Curry were both very much Christians. They didn't swear and were good-living men. Jimmy Murphy had the patience of Job with the youngsters, and Bert Whalley was the same. He was brilliant.

'Tom Curry was a wonderfully kind person. He never shouted at people to get things done. Sometimes we used to pull his leg by turning up for training and saying, "We're doing nothing for you this morning". And we'd all walk in a line and pretend to be completely disinterested.

'"Ah, come on lads," Tom would say in that wonderfully warm way he had. "You'll do it for me, won't you?" And we did, of course.

'The day I first appeared for United after signing from Doncaster, Matt Busby left out five players and put them in the reserves against Barnsley. It was amazing, because that meant there were ten internationals in the reserve team that day and eleven in the first team playing Leicester at Old Trafford.

'After Munich I played with a United side that did a job. Players like Stan Crowther and Maurice Setters and Ernie Taylor did their best, of course, but it was never the same United after Munich.

'Pre-Munich it was the best club in the world. In 1957 no one could compete with Real Madrid. But a year later we had matured a great deal and were ready to take them.'

Wilf McGuinness, destined in 1969 to be chosen from the United family as Matt Busby's successor and to experience a harrowing start to his managerial career, has now returned to Cheshire after a heartening period of rehabilitation in Greek football. After two years with Aris, Salonika, and a year with Panahaiki, he was enjoying a break and waiting for the right opportunity to reshape his career in England.

His playing days ended in 1960, when he broke a leg, but his standards were clear because he was a man who had grown up with greatness and had no wish to forget it. 'I often think about that time and the team we had in the 1950s,' he said. 'And I love talking about it, because it gives me pleasure, not sadness.

'When I remember those players and, perhaps most important of all, the unbelievable team spirit at the club then, I feel the whole period gives us something we can still aim for. For me, it is something to aim for as a manager. To look for the kind of players who could do the sort of things those players could do, even though I know I could never find them. But somewhere, by striving, I might just catch glimpses here and there and that will be something.

'After Munich I got a couple of England caps, but, to try to put myself in perspective, let me say that I was not fit to polish the boots of Duncan Edwards and Eddie Colman. To be a reserve to them was something special. Every player in that team had something extra and the spirit within that team helped to make Manchester United what it was.

'Before Munich I got a League Championship medal as a reserve, having played fourteen first team games, but I never felt that I was anything special. I was just lucky to be around that great team.

'I used to read press cuttings and perhaps I'd get a mention ". . . and McGuinness helped make the goal". I would have to smile, because what I had done, most likely, was to have given the ball to someone like Billy Whelan and then watched as he and others developed a move and finished it off.

'After the crash it was tremendous how the team picked up. It was something superhuman, because we were not that great as a team. But we managed somehow, with lads like Harry Gregg, Ian Greaves, Freddie Goodwin, myself, Albert

Scanlon and, mainly, Dennis Viollet, Bobby Charlton, Warren Bradley and, to a certain extent, Albert Quixall. It was always the case at United that the players would give everything.

'Shortly before the Belgrade trip I damaged a cartilage and was waiting for an operation, so I didn't travel that time.

'Jimmy Murphy did tremendously well. He had to keep things going. It was a job that required someone very strong and I don't think anyone else but Jimmy could have done it. But I know he spent every minute of every day and night working things out.

'He bought Stan Crowther because we were short of wing halves and I played a couple of games five weeks after the operation. There was a lot of young talent at the club, but a lot of the boys had to be put into the team before they were really ready. Before their time.

'Lads like Mark Pearson and Alex Dawson did well in the circumstances, but some of the other boys were not ready for the demands that had to be placed upon them.

'A great period had ended. A great team was finished before it had really blossomed, and there has not been better. Times have changed. Everyone saw United's success at bringing youngsters through and started youth policies of their own.

'It still goes on, but fewer youngsters seem to come through and the transfer market has become the big thing. Success has to be bought. But, as I say, my experience of the great days has given me something to aim for. When I think back about my time at United I don't think of the recent past, I think of the great past.'

Ken Morgans left United for his native Swansea at the start of the 1960s and five years later was transferred to Newport. The right winger retired from football at thirty, and is now a publican, at the Lower New Inn, Pontypool.

'I think the way the club progressed after the crash was just one of those things,' he said. 'Players from the "A" team and the reserves put up a fantastic show and Jimmy Murphy was there to keep everything going.

'Only Jimmy could have done it. He had a way of talking to players. He could have put a fifteen-year-old in that team and he would have been a success.

'I got back before the FA Cup semi-final and played against Liverpool in the reserves and then in the first team against Portsmouth when the team had just won the semi-final.

'There was a tremendous amount of interest in the team, of course, but we had that even before the crash. We were used to living with that. Even before Munich it would take an hour and a half to get out of a ground after a game.

'Our style was attractive to watch. We had Duncan and Eddie at wing half and when we were attacking they would move up to make seven forwards. Then Roger would move up to make eight – and what forwards they were! And if we were defending, the wingers would go back to become extra full backs.

'But times change, and times changed for United after they had been on top for so many years. When the greats like Matt Busby and Jimmy Murphy retired I was not interested any more. A few years ago I could tell you every player at the club. Ask me to name four players now and I couldn't do it.'

On Monday 15 July, 1974, Jackie Blanchflower was back at hospital for another operation on his right arm, injured at Munich and still causing him pain.

'I thought the arm was going to be the least of my injuries immediately after the crash,' said Jackie, 'but that just goes to show how wrong you can be.'

Blanchflower never played after Munich, and recalled: 'When I came back my future was in the hands of specialists. I saw three and finally I was convinced that football was out of the question.

'It was a load off my mind, but it was also a big disappointment. My wife Jean says I am bitter, but I don't think so really. I became depressed and did nothing for a couple of years. It was not that I couldn't do anything. I just did not want to do anything.

'I was twenty-five, an ex-professional footballer out of work. Eventually I had to get a job and I worked for a bookmaker for eight years. It was six years ago that I took over the pub.'

The Blanchflowers took over the Royal Oak at Millbrook, near Stalybridge, some ten miles from Manchester.

'I don't think football is as good today as when we played,' he said. 'We used to all go up the field attacking together and all go back defending together. And we were always most dangerous when we were being attacked, because we could break out very effectively and take advantage of the gaps opponents left.

'There's too much theory about the game these days. Too much tactical stuff and too much coaching,' said the man who played in every position for United except outside right – 'I was just never picked there' – and, after making an emergency appearance in goal when Ray Wood was injured in the 1957 FA Cup Final, he was actually selected as goalkeeper for a tour match in Sweden. ('We won easily and I never touched the ball.')

But in spite of such versatility, he was never able to make any one position his own.

'I was a Jack of all trades, and it was amazing how each time I thought I was establishing myself in a particular position I would go to play for Ireland and the player who took my place at United would have a blinder and I'd be left out again. This happened on three occasions.

'After Munich the team pulled itself round very well but this did not surprise me greatly because the club still had enough good players left to do the job. Players like Bobby Charlton, Dennis Viollet and Harry Gregg. And Ernie Taylor, who was bought, did a good job for them.

'I've always maintained that if you have four or five great

194

players you will have a successful team. But it took a while for things to come right again for United, to get on some kind of level similar to the one before Munich, because Matt Busby was ill for a long, long time after the crash, even when he was back in charge. I don't think it is realized fully how ill Matt was when he came back.

'When United were relegated I was not surprised because it had been coming for a couple of years. It has happened to other great clubs in the past and that's how the game is. It goes in cycles. The only thing to do is to start again.

'We used to have a tremendous spirit at the club when I was playing and we also had a sense of humour. That is very important.

'I think we all believe we are indispensable but none of us is and it comes as a big disappointment when we find that out.

'Those days in the 1950s were very special and I made up something myself to try to show how I felt about those boys: "What we have lost they have gained in respect and immortality".'

Albert Scanlon is now a docker. The man once noted for his speed down the left flank at Old Trafford is now 'Pockets' to his fellow dockers. All his workmates have nicknames and Albert's came easily on the day he first reported for duty. It was freezing cold and Albert stood around all day with his hands in his pockets.

Down at the docks you do not ask for Alf because there are many Alfs and the one you want may be 'Flat Nose Alf'. Among other colourful characters are 'Freddy the Frog' and a couple of lads known as 'The Railway Children' in this Damon Runyon part of Manchester.

'I like working at the docks because here it's like being a part of a big family,' said Albert.

'After Munich I spent another two years at Old Trafford, had about twelve months at Newcastle, two years at Lincoln and three good years at Mansfield. It was never the same after United, but my time at Mansfield came closest to being in any way similar.

'The atmosphere there was good and the manager, Tommy Cummings, had brought with him a style and attitude from his days at Burnley.

'After Mansfield, I stopped playing and had to look for a job for the first time in my life. I didn't know anything else.

'First, I worked in a bakery and then I tried a factory. It was no good. I could not settle. But then I went down to the docks and found I enjoyed the life.

'One of the lads at the docks said one day that he would have given his right arm to have done what I did. One of the other lads asked what I had done that was so special and I told him that I had played for United in the great days and travelled all over Europe, visiting most of the capitals, and America, living first class all the time.

'If I suddenly became a millionaire and went to all those places again it would not be the same, because, best of all, I travelled with the people I wanted to travel with. Now I have my memories, something that cannot be taken away from me. And I'm happy. I'm grateful to have played for United and to have got out of that aircraft alive.

'I grew up in Hulme, Manchester, which is Manchester City territory, and I remember one day Johnny Carey visited our school to make a presentation. I was introduced to him and he asked in front of all the other boys what was my ambition. "To play for United," I said, and everyone laughed. But I realized my ambition.

'My wife works nights to help out and sometimes when I'm in the house on my own I'll go through matches from the old days in my mind or just think about some of the great times we had. I can remember everything from my first day at Old Trafford.

'I started on the ground staff and became the tea boy. You

would never go barging into the first team dressing room. You had to have respect for everyone. One of my first promotions was to lay out the kit in the dressing rooms.

'The difference between the first team dressing room and the second team dressing room was amazing. You would go into the first team dressing room and lay out all the kit in the right place, all neatly. I can still remember where each of those great players, Carey, Rowley and the rest, would be in the dressing room.

'But you would stumble into the reserve dressing room under a whole mixed up mass of gear and just plonk it down and let them dive in for it.

'One of the biggest thrills of my life was when I got my first United blazer to go on a youth tour to Ireland. I stopped people to see how they thought it looked on me.

'I was nearly twenty-two when I finally got into the first team on anything like a regular basis, but I enjoyed my whole time at the club. The lads used to call me "Joe Friday" after a character in the television detective series "Dragnet", because if anything was going on, I'd always be around.

'After Munich, I think there were three or four reasons why the club was able to pull itself together.

'The players excelled themselves. Jimmy Murphy took everything upon himself and was helped by Jack Crompton and Ted Dalton, among others. Ernie Taylor was thrown in among it all and fitted in so well. And Les Olive made an amazing transition from assistant to club secretary.

'I played with Les when he was a goalkeeper in the "A" team, "B" team and reserves. When I went to Yugoslavia Les was just an assistant. When I came back he had taken everything on and that must have been a terrible jump for him.

'I'm still a United supporter and I was very upset when they went down last year. It was just their turn to have a run of bad luck.

'I sat through one game at Old Trafford last year, when United were beaten when they should have won, and I ended up reading a book. I just couldn't watch any longer.

'I always felt lucky to play with United at the time I did. People have said I played at the wrong time because of the money that came into the game for players later. But they haven't got the memories. I don't begrudge anybody anything. I'm just happy to have been around at the time I was.

'The kids who follow United now are fanatics, but I believe the fanaticism stemmed from that day in Munich.

'A team died, but I believe a club was born.'

15. Captain Thain

It took Captain James Thain eleven years and four inquiries, two German, two British, to clear his name of blame for the Munich air disaster and he has not flown an aircraft since that fateful day, 6 February 1958.

The first inquiry, in West Germany, decided that the crash was caused by ice on the wings of the aircraft, which resulted in Captain Thain being blamed because that was his responsibility. Captain Thain was dissatisfied with the way this inquiry was conducted and disagreed with its findings.

He believed the crash was caused by slush on the runway and sought a new inquiry, which was held in April 1960, by the Fay Commission. This tribunal, like the one in Germany, decided the crash had been caused by ice on the wings.

On Christmas morning, 1960, Captain Thain received notification of his dismissal from British European Airways for a breach of their regulations in that he had changed seats with his first officer. Captain Kenneth Rayment flew the aircraft from Belgrade from the left-hand seat. Captain Thain occupied the right-hand seat. It is quite in order for the captain to permit his first officer to fly the aircraft provided the first officer is fully qualified. The first officer can act as 'pilot in charge' and fly the plane while the captain takes the role of co-pilot, but the captain remains in command.

However, BEA forbade the captain and first officer to change seats, insisting that the captain remain in the left-hand seat. But Captain Thain, acting as co-pilot from the left-hand seat, found it more difficult to monitor the instruments because they were not duplicated in front of him.

This breach of BEA regulations, coupled with the fact that he did not check the Elizabethan's wings physically for ice traces, resulted in Captain Thain's dismissal from the company. He was not reinstated.

Captain Thain and Captain Rayment were friends and near neighbours. Captain Thain had decided to invest money in poultry farming. Captain Rayment heard about the venture and was keen to get a more detailed breakdown of how it worked.

'Around this time BEA wanted a pilot and first officer for a charter flight from Manchester to Belgrade,' said Captain Thain. 'I was called by the administrative officer of the Elizabethan flight and offered the "plum trip". I wasn't particularly keen on it and would have been quite happy if someone else had taken it.

'At this time Ken was just fit again following an illness, a hernia operation. He was keen to do some flying again and to hear about the poultry farm. I liked the idea of having his company and told him "I've got this charter of a football team. Manchester City or United. (I was not clear which because I was not a follower of football.) Why don't you see if you can get it?"

'Ken thought it was a good idea, and it was put to the flight administration officer to roster Ken as first officer, but somebody else had already been rostered for this trip, so he was made a standby. It turned out that the chap who should have been first officer had just returned from duty in Malta and opted for two days' leave which was due to him.

'When I arrived to collect the charter plane, Ken was there. I said, "Right, I'll take her to Belgrade and you can bring her back". He said that was fine, so that's the way we worked. I must emphasize that we were both fully qualified pilots and both captains. In fact, Ken had more flying time in Elizabethans than I had (3143 hours against 1722).

'BEA introduced the regulation about the seats after an accident involving a Dakota some time earlier. They insisted that the pilot in command should always sit in the left-hand seat, the seat to which he was accustomed. As a captain, Ken Rayment was accustomed to the left-hand seat. And I had satisfied myself that the wings were free of any ice hazard.'

Captain Thain's claims that slush had caused the Munich crash were reinforced by an aviation incident in the United States. A Boeing 707 came out of a warm hangar with dry wings and was taken straight down a runway for take-off. There was slush on the runway and when the aircraft passed 'V1', the last point for safe abandonment of take-off, the pilot noticed a drastic deceleration, even without any loss of power from the engines. The aircraft became airborne – but clearing a hedge at the end of the runway by only five feet.

'The Americans held an immediate inquiry and decided to reconstruct the take-off,' said Captain Thain. 'They did so, successfully, with American style. They used ice-making machines to reproduce conditions similar to those at the time the Boeing came out of the hangar and had film cameras everywhere, including helicopters over the runway.

'When the experimental aircraft, Convair 880, reached the same point of the runway, there was deceleration again, and intensive studies of the results of these findings established slush as a major hazard. When I heard about this, it was a breakthrough, and tests were later carried out with an Elizabethan by the Royal Aeronautical Establishment for the then Board of Trade at Bedford. And these bore out the American findings.

'They proved that an aircraft taking off with slush on the runway was subject to drag forces which were so great that they could cause the aircraft to slow down enough to prevent it from being able to take off. This is what happened to the Elizabethan at Munich.'

The new factor eventually led to a second German inquiry, opened in accordance with Annex 13 of the International Civil Aviation Organisation (ICAO), the internationally recognized procedure for aircraft accident investigation. This recommends that an inquiry should be re-opened if new and significant evidence comes to light which is likely to produce a change in the original findings.

'But the second German inquiry began by stating that they accepted the findings of the first inquiry as their basis for their new inquiry and would only hear the new evidence on slush,' said Captain Thain.

The Germans stuck to their original decision about ice on the wings, in spite of the experiments in the United States and at Bedford. Said Captain Thain: 'When the report of this second German inquiry arrived at the Board of Trade it was so full of contradictions and mistakes that the Ministry were in a dilemma. The Board of Trade could not accept a lot that was in the German report but failed to get them to change their minds.

'In the end, the report was published in the United Kingdom, but with the report of the Royal Aircraft Establishment attached, which completely contradicted the Germans' case. It was agreed to hold a second British inquiry. In fact, after hoping for this for years, I finally had one hour twenty minutes to agree to the new inquiry. The only snag as far as I could see was that the inquiry would be conducted by the same tribunal as the original one, the Fay Commission.

'I felt I had to talk with the lawyers of the British Airline Pilots' Association for a legal opinion on the terms of reference of the tribunal, whether it might be inhibited by the findings of the first British inquiry. Our QC, John May, reassured me that there was no reason why the commission could not reverse the decision of the first British inquiry. So I said, "Yes, please".'

In June 1969 Captain Thain, then forty-seven, was cleared publicly when a statement was read in the House of Commons. The British Airline Pilots' Association had spent around £12,000 on legal fees, and a member had been cleared on an important technical point.

Looking back in 1974, Captain Thain said: 'I gave up in

1969. It was as far as I could go without sacrificing my family. I had to draw a line somewhere. I was cleared of blame after eleven years, but it did not make any difference.

'My licence had expired. I had been dismissed *without justification* and I was not reinstated. I was the Winslow Boy of aviation. I had to fight my own case. I was happy to leave it all to the experts, but they did not find the real cause of the accident. I fought to clear my name, and I have achieved that in the eyes of the aviation world. I might have been better off if I had accepted the original findings and kept my licence and tried to get a job flying elsewhere. I am too far down the runway to be able to fly now, but I was robbed of my profession. That's what has hit me most. I have been unable to settle to anything else. I feel let down.'

Captain Thain's home, Hayley Green Farm, is at the heart of a lush, green Berkshire triangle of Windsor, Ascot and Bracknell. Overhead were the sounds of frequent aircraft, journeying to or from nearby Heathrow Airport. 'I do sometimes look up at one and gauge its altitude and speed and think "That should be me up there flying that".'

He had given up farming and, at fifty-two, became involved in some property development. 'I got out of farming to avoid bankruptcy,' he said. 'It was that bad. People do not seem to realize how difficult it can be for farmers today with costs rising all the time. If it were not for the increased value of their homes they would not survive. Whatever I came to be worth came just by having the place, not by the efforts I put into farming.'

To raise capital he had sold his fifteenth-century house with a moat and had built a bungalow on to a cottage at the front of his land.

Mrs Ruby Thain backed her husband's fight. She had science degrees in chemistry and physics, was teaching at a local convent school, and later moved to a technical college where she lectured on nutrition.

'The biggest effect the whole thing has had on me was it

meant I had to continue teaching. It changed our whole pattern of life. Even all the work we did on the farm came to nothing in the end. By now we would have been in a position to retire and enjoy what was left of our lives,' she said.

Sebuda Thain, the Captain's attractive blonde daughter, who is a teacher of physical instruction and general subjects, was married in July 1974. 'I remember all the reporters coming to the house and the other children at school talking about how life was for them. I would just say, "Oh, our life is different".

'I teach at a mixed school and the boys often talk about football. Sometimes I'm asked, "Which team do you support, Miss?" and I tell them Manchester United.'

Captain Thain had kept in touch with Captain Rayment's widow, Mary. 'Ken's son, Stephen, was a young lad at the time and got some kind of job in BEA. But he had no qualifications and though he wanted to become a pilot there was no chance of this happening the way things were,' said Captain Thain.

'I telephoned Mary one day and asked if Stephen was there. She said he was in the bath and warned me that he did not think too highly of me. He had a resentment against me, and I think he'd heard things about me whilst working for BEA that were not very complimentary. This disturbed me, and I asked Mary to tell Stephen that I would very much like to see him for a chat and that he could call at my house whenever he liked.

'He did come and I said, "Right, Stephen, let's sit down and talk about the whole thing and you can hear my side of the story". He did, and said it made a big change in his attitude. I also told him that his chances of getting a pilot's licence in this country were very slim because of his lack of qualifications and advised him to try abroad. He is now flying for an oil company in the Middle East, and we still see each other from time to time.'

Captain Thain had taken more notice of football since

1958. 'I'm not an enthusiast, but I do watch matches when they are on television,' he said. 'Particularly Manchester United, though when I do it all comes back to me. That's inevitable, I suppose.

'I went to a game at Old Trafford some time ago, though I can't even remember who United were playing. I had gone to visit a friend at Mytholmroyd, near Hebden Bridge, and he said United were playing a home game and suggested we went to the match. We sat in the stand and just left with the other spectators at the end of the game. I saw the memorial at the main entrance.

'One day I received a call from a friend, Tim Yates, the chairman of Shrewsbury Town. His club was staying at a hotel in Ascot to break a journey to play at Brighton. Harry Gregg was the Shrewsbury manager at the time and Tim invited me out to Ascot to meet him. We had a long chat, and he struck me as being a nice chap.'

He added: 'I don't feel responsible in any way for the crash. Twenty-three people died and it was a terrible tragedy, something that will always be with me. It must be the most publicized air crash of all time, because it involved a famous football team.

'But if I had died at Munich there is no doubt in my mind that it would have been accepted that the crash had been caused by ice on the wings and the dangers of the slush hazard would not have been realized so soon.

'How many more people might have lost their lives if I had not been able to battle on?'

16. Transition

When Manchester United were relegated for the first time in thirty-six years, sandwiched between Norwich City and Southampton at the end of the inaugural three-up-three-down season of 1973–4, they were the best supported football team in Britain. Their fall was witnessed by a total attendance of 1,012,253 for all matches played at Old Trafford and a total nationwide audience, home and away, of 1,754,672.

Apart from a splendid flourish to take ten points from twelve, which gave their supporters hope in the twilight of the season, there was only frustration and disappointment for the faithful who stayed loyal all the way down to the Second Division.

It was a successful time for some. Leeds United held off a strong challenge by Liverpool and won the League Championship. Liverpool overran an ineffectual Newcastle United to win the FA Cup. Jack Charlton's first season as a manager saw Middlesbrough canter to the Second Division championship, and Carlisle United won a place in the First Division.

For others it was a time of uncertainty. Sir Alf Ramsey was sacked as England's team manager, Don Revie leaving Leeds to take his place. Brian Clough left Brighton to take Revie's job at Leeds, and was sacked after forty-four days. Malcolm Allison, the master coach during years of plenty at Manchester City, slipped into the Third Division with Crystal Palace. Bobby Charlton found himself in the Third Division with Preston after his first season as a manager. Bill Shankly stunned Merseyside by retiring as the manager of Liverpool, the job going to his assistant, Bob Paisley.

United were in a state of transition. Charlton had left; Denis Law had gone to Manchester City on a free transfer, had played for Scotland in the World Cup finals in West Germany and had then retired; George Best, back until Christmas, quit for a third time (next stop Dunstable in the Southern League); injury ended the career of Ian Moore.

The manager, Tommy Docherty, had saved the club from relegation the previous year by utilising his experience as the Scotland team manager to prop up the team by signing several of his countrymen. Soon only two Englishmen, Alex Stepney and Brian Greenhoff, and three Irishmen, Sammy McIlroy, Gerry Daly and Mick Martin, could offer an alternative to the Scottish accent.

When Docherty failed to keep United afloat a second time, some people outside the club took the attitude that demotion would prove to be beneficial in the long term, and facts were facts: if you did not win enough points, you went down; no club had a divine right to First Division football.

Docherty said he knew that a lot of people, envious of the club, were delighted to see them go down, but emphasized that a pattern was emerging, with young players coming through to assure the club of a bright future. 'Above all,' he said, 'our supporters are fantastic.' But a hard core of these was not, rampaging through cities and towns, damaging persons and properties. All clubs had a hooligan element, but United's fame attracted more than most.

Along with the hooligans, and adding to the problem, were high-spirited youngsters simply 'joining in'. United's last home game of the season, a farewell to the First Division, was disrupted by pitch invasions by youngsters after Law had scored the only goal for Manchester City minutes from the end. United's last game, away to Stoke City, was also marred by their young followers, who threw lighted papers and scarves among the crowd on the terraces. Before United played a match in the Second Division, fences were erected behind each goal at Old Trafford to discourage

207

further pitch invasions, and these were later extended round the ground.

Sir Matt Busby was still there, working from an office at the end of a corridor from the manager's room. Many people believed he should have left with his memories years before, to be revered in retrospect for a job well done. It was argued by some that, in time, a man not only outlives his usefulness but can inhibit progress merely by being seen to remain in orbit.

Creative men are not easily parted from their life's work, and the former pit boy from Orbiston, Lanarkshire, who had played wing half for Manchester City and Liverpool, had captained and later managed Scotland, and had spent twenty-three years converting a bomb site into a Mecca, felt he still had a contribution to make at sixty-five.

In 1969, having retired as the manager following triumph in the European Cup, Busby became the general manager. In 1971 he was made a director, and football in general decided it was time that full use was made of his statesmanship and diplomacy and he was appointed a member of the Football Association's International Committee, the body responsible for the England team. He was later made United's president.

He was knighted in 1968, having been honoured with a CBE in 1958, and was also made a Knight Commander of St Gregory and a Freeman of Manchester. A time for accolades. A time, also, for problems.

When Busby, his dream fulfilled, decided to offer the manager's chair to a younger man, his third great team was waning as a unit, even though it contained exceptional individual players such as Charlton, Law and Best.

The choice of successor came from within 'the family': Wilf McGuinness, the former 'Babe' whose playing career was ended by injury. McGuinness's problem was that he was contemporary with the team, and he was judged a failure after a season in which he almost took United to Wembley. He was demoted and finally left the club.

Busby took charge of the team again while searching for another manager, and the 1971–2 season opened with the Irishman Frank O'Farrell in the job. O'Farrell lasted a season and a half, starting with spectacular results, spending £600,000 and leaving with the team on the verge of the Second Division.

During this period George Best began to lose interest in the game. Having shown a tendency in the latter part of Busby's time towards wayward behaviour off the field by missing trains to matches, enjoying a widely publicized love life and lingering in night clubs, this great player almost carried the team with his skill and goals at the start of O'Farrell's reign. But he was finding it more difficult to combine his lifestyle with the strain of sustaining a diminishing talent.

Best quit twice, the second occasion coinciding with O'Farrell's dismissal. Tommy Docherty moved in, saved the club from relegation in the spring of 1973 and helped Best fight his way back to another comeback, which ended with a third 'retirement'.

When I talked to Busby in his office in the summer of 1974, a telephone rang out an interruption, and he made a note of another appointment. 'I'm on the committee planning the Lancashire new town around the Preston area,' he said. 'I got involved in that a couple of years ago, when Julian Amery was Minister of the Environment. He called me one day and said he wanted me on the committee. I said I wasn't sure about it, but he insisted, so there we were.'

The 1973–4 fixture list, a grim reminder, had been removed from the wall of the office, and the one ready to take its place, appointments with unfamiliar opponents such as Oldham Athletic and York City, promised only uncertainty. 'It was disappointing to go down,' Busby said, 'but towards the end of the season a pattern of play began to emerge again and this gave us confidence for the future.

'The young players did well, boys like Brian Greenhoff and Gerry Daly and Sammy McIlroy. Willie Morgan has been with us for some time, but has always looked after himself so well, and we have bought Stuart Pearson from Hull and hope he will be the man to round things off, to bring the goals we lacked before and take a little bit of weight off the boys around him so that they will have a better chance of goals, too.'

It would take more than demotion to dispirit the man who came back from an oxygen tent at the Rechts der Isar Hospital to build again.

Jimmy Murphy was also still to be found at Old Trafford, though now he worked on a part-time basis and spent a lot of time out and about watching matches in the endless search for talent. Often he would go to the ground in the morning, put on his track suit, do a spot of training on his own to keep fit, then have a shower and perhaps take a walk round the pitch.

He was 'sad but optimistic' about the club's position, and out there in the stadium Murphy was never far from a million memories of the great games of the past. He could readily call to mind Duncan Edwards ('He was not just a player, he was a *team*') and could see the boys moving forward with a simple, effective, entertaining style. 'The hardest part of the game is to win the ball. Once you have won it, you attack, going forward, not across or back, and when an attack breaks down, as they do, each player picks up an opponent and defends.'

It has been said that Manchester United have something far more potent than success – they have folklore. Many people took the club to heart in 1958.

Chris Fiddler, who cried on 6 February 1958, was now a civil servant in Manchester and a member of the United Supporters' Club. 'I didn't really appreciate how good the team was before the crash,' he said. 'I was just fourteen and watching football. The deeper feelings came later. After the crash I was drawn closer to the club in a way. From being sixteen I started to go to every match, and when United won the European Cup I thought, "That's what they've been playing for all those years". It came home to me that it was a sort of fulfilment of what the old team had set out to achieve. I expected the club to go down last season, but I'll be there, home and away, and most of the people I know will be there, too.'

Anne Gilliland, the girl whose interest in football brought her trouble at school, had become Mrs Anne Smith, a founder member, with her husband David, of the Manchester United Supporters' Club. David became the chairman, Anne the secretary. She had also become a part-time physical education teacher at her old school, The Hollies.

'Yes, things have turned full circle from my younger days – even the head is a keen United supporter now,' she said. 'United trained on our school playing fields once and a party from the school had a look round Old Trafford.

'At the moment I feel optimistic. I don't think there is a lot of difference between the teams at the bottom of the First Division and those at the top of the Second. I think we can come straight back up again.

'United fans are different from all the others, you can see that from the attendances when we were at the bottom of the First Division. It's a very special club.

'Winning the European Cup in 1968 was for the lads of 1958. We talked about it on the train coming back from Wembley. Those people who didn't go to United before Munich don't know the potential of that team. It was a team full of stars rather than a team with a star. Perhaps this is the secret of the club's support. Perhaps people are waiting for this to happen again. There is a standard to aim for. You couldn't have a higher standard.

'The pre-Munich supporters who still go to Old Trafford

will not stand for any United team since those days being compared with the team of the 1950s. To the older fans there was only one team called "The Babes".'

Anne Smith, Chris Fiddler and thousands like them had hope, but was there something more tangible for them to cling to? The bookmakers made United odds-on favourites for promotion in the 1974–5 season, no doubt impressed by the team's flourish towards the end of the previous season and confident that the club's tradition would guarantee whole-hearted support.

As always, everything depended upon the quality of the players, men such as Alex Stepney in goal, Martin Buchan and Jim Holton, encouraged by their splendid efforts for Scotland's World Cup team in West Germany, and Willie Morgan, whose performances for Scotland were a continuation of his high level of consistency for his club.

The thoughts of the old scout, Joe Armstrong, still centred on the club he had helped to build. He would tell you that his first signing was Jeff Whitefoot from Stockport; then came Dennis Viollet and Mark Jones, and his greatest capture was a boy from Ashington called Bobby Charlton, though Duncan Edwards 'was the greatest schoolboy player of all time'.

Joe's love for United was still so strong that, although retired, he felt in some way responsible for the club's decline and subsequent relegation. Putting aside all the years of bountiful harvest, he said: 'I blame myself partly because I brought a lot of the players to the club and recently we have not had as much success with youngsters.

'I've always said you can't find winners all the time and for each success you are bound to have failures. But I've always loved watching schoolboy players, watching for abilities – skill in the feet, the will to go, speed and strength – that tell me a boy has potential.

'It was sad that United went down, but I'm confident they will come back up again soon and I just wish I was starting out all over again looking for young players. I am sure more star players will come through soon. All my life in football I have believed in the future. I have said, "There was Meredith . . . but behind him came Matthews".'

Joe died in March 1975, three weeks short of his eighty-first birthday, secure in the knowledge that his beloved United were on their way back to the top flight. The scout's faith in the club was justified. United attacked the Second Division with verve from August 1974 through to May 1975, displaying the impatience of a team which had no time to linger.

They came straight back to the First Division with sixty-one points, which gave them the Second Division championship, three points ahead of Aston Villa and eight points ahead of Norwich City, both of whom were also promoted. Moreover, United's support during the brief visit to the Second Division had proved to be as massive, as intense and as fearsome as ever.

Captain James Thain, the man in charge of the ill-fated Elizabethan on 6 February 1958, died on 6 August 1975, ten days before United started life afresh in the First Division with a 2–0 victory at Wolverhampton. Captain Thain, who was fifty-three, had suffered from heart trouble.

Sceptics doubted that Docherty's team had either the strength or the experience to challenge for honours in the First Division, and were confounded when United were serious contenders for the League title until mid-April and went on to reach the FA Cup Final. On this occasion they were defeated by Southampton, a Second Division club, the only goal of the match being scored by Bobby Stokes towards the end of the second half.

The following year, United returned to Wembley and won the FA Cup, thereby frustrating Liverpool's attempt to achieve a 'treble' of the League Championship, the FA Cup and the European Cup. The match was settled in United's favour, 2–1, when a shot by Jimmy Greenhoff took a deflection into the Liverpool goal after the Merseysiders had equalized, Jimmy Case squaring the game following a strike by Stuart Pearson.

Docherty's triumph had scarcely been celebrated before the manager was dismissed from office following revelations of an affair with Mary Brown, the wife of the club's physiotherapist. While the popular Scot continued his nomadic career through football, courting controversy, United turned to Dave Sexton, a Trappist by comparison.

The taciturn Sexton, who had gained a reputation for team planning as the manager of Chelsea and Queen's Park Rangers in turn, brought a measured approach to a side Docherty had built adventurously. Under Sexton's guidance, United reached the FA Cup Final again in 1979, losing to Arsenal 3–2. In a frantic finish, Gordon McQueen and Sammy McIlroy put United level after Brian Talbot and Frank Stapleton had given Arsenal what seemed an unassailable lead. With seconds remaining, and United's supporters keenly anticipating extra time, Alan Sunderland scored the winning goal.

It was during this period that Harry Gregg made a reappearance at Old Trafford to coach the club's goalkeepers. Some time later, a visit to England was paid by Vesag Lukic, whom Gregg had rescued from the wrecked aircraft in Munich when she was a two-year-old travelling with her mother to join her father at the Yugoslavian Embassy in London.

Sexton's position was insecure even though he nudged the team to finish two points behind Liverpool, the champions, in the 1979–80 season. A year later, he was informed by Martin Edwards, who had become United's chairman on the death of his father, Louis, in 1980, that he was fired. Sexton left club football to coach England's fledgling international players at the FA's School of Excellence.

On failing to lure either Bobby Robson from Ipswich Town or Lawrie McMenemy from Southampton, United recruited the bejewelled Ron Atkinson from West Bromwich Albion.

Atkinson persuaded his former club to accept a record £1.5m for Bryan Robson, and United began to play in an attractive, attacking style.

Atkinson's team twice won the FA Cup, defeating Brighton, 4–0, in a replay in 1983 with two goals by Robson and one each by Norman Whiteside and Arnold Muhren, and beating Everton, 1–0, in 1985 thanks to an inspired piece of marksmanship by Whiteside after Kevin Moran had made Cup Final history by being sent off.

By now the club's craving for the League Championship was intense; after all, man had been to the moon since the trophy was last brought to Old Trafford by Busby in 1967. Atkinson was unable to deliver it, and in 1986 he suffered a fate similar to that of his predecessor. At this point United placed the team in the care of Alex Ferguson, who had achieved enormous success in domestic and European competitions as the manager of Aberdeen and had also sampled life in charge of Scotland's World Cup squad.

Epilogue

Jimmy Murphy, who kept the flag flying at Old Trafford during the harrowing days of 1958, died on 15 November 1989, aged 79. Murphy assisted Matt Busby in establishing a mode of team management others tried to emulate with varying degrees of success.

On arriving at Manchester United Alex Ferguson, like Busby an advocate of nurturing young talent, set about revitalizing the club's youth-development programme. In common with Wilf McGuinness, Frank O'Farrell, Tommy Docherty, Dave Sexton and Ron Atkinson before him, however, the new manager had the problem of pressure demanding instant success. Moreover, Ferguson's appointment coincided with the hardening of a financial philosophy which was about to envelop the game.

The foundations of football's transformation from a professional sport to a commercial operation had been prepared down the years, words such as 'consumer' and 'product' gradually supplanting 'supporter' and 'game'. A number of affluent clubs clamoured for a 'super league', or super market, in which to increase their profits, particularly from television revenue. By the 1990s, the flotation of football clubs was burgeoning, and it was Manchester United plc's business to be to the fore, on the field and on the stock exchange.

Football-team management is not a serene occupation. It is worth recounting that even Busby's reign did not escape rumour and speculation. After three consecutive defeats in the 1950–1 season, the headline I'M NOT GETTING THE SACK appeared above an article that carried Busby's name in the

16 January 1951 issue of *All Football.* Fifteen months later, Busby won the first of his five League titles.

Ferguson had to endure a campaign launched against him in 1989 by disaffected United supporters. A 1–0 win at Nottingham Forest in the third round of the FA Cup in 1990 is often cited as saving Ferguson's job. Victory against Crystal Palace in a replay of the FA Cup Final restored a spirit of optimism.

This was heightened in May 1991 when United won the European Cup Winners Cup, a major achievement for English football as well as for the club. Six years had elapsed since UEFA had closed its competitions to English clubs after the Heysel Stadium disaster in Brussels, when thirty-nine died in a riot before the start of the European Cup Final between Juventus and Liverpool.

While United's success in the Cup Winners Cup hardly compared with their 1968 triumph in the Champions Cup, which carried the prestige of Europe's premier tournament and the emotion of a promise fulfilled, it had sufficient merit to convince the sceptics that Ferguson was the man to galvanize the club.

The final, played at the Feyenoord Stadium in Rotterdam, was against Barcelona, fresh from winning the Spanish championship and coached by the illustrious Dutchman Johan Cruyff. United prevailed 2–1.

Mark Hughes, whose skill and heroic determination made him a favourite of United's followers, proved sharper than Cruyff's players on the night. The Welshman added a touch to Steve Bruce's goal-bound header following a Bryan Robson free kick after 68 minutes, and scored the second goal six minutes later.

It was United's 100th goal of the season, and one of particular personal satisfaction for Hughes in view of the mixed fortunes he experienced during his time at Barcelona. Ronald Koeman scored for the Spanish side from a free kick after 80 minutes, from which point United were under intense pressure. 'The last ten minutes was like ten years,' Ferguson said.

A wet, blustery evening did not dampen the spirit of the spectators, and although security was tight there was a lighter side to the operation. A dog-handler at the United end, for example, tethered his Alsatian to a fence, which he then proceeded to climb in order to drape a Union Jack passed to him through the railings. For United, the festival of the 1990s was just beginning.

Adjustments continued to be made. Archie Knox, Ferguson's no. 2, returned to Scotland. He was replaced by Brian Kidd, back home at Old Trafford after adding to his experience with Arsenal, Manchester City, Bolton and several clubs in the United States before turning to coaching at Barrow, Swindon and Preston.

Kidd, who had marked his nineteenth birthday at the 1968 European Cup Final by scoring the third of United's four goals against Benfica, rejoined the club in 1988. He graduated from coaching the juniors, directing the school of excellence and serving as the youth-development officer to become Ferguson's answer to Jimmy Murphy.

United proved to be well equipped for the advent of a lucrative super league, which materialized in season 1992–3 as the old First Division became the FA Premier League, and football on TV was restyled by satellite television.

Having watched his team finish the previous season as runners-up to Leeds United, Ferguson managed to acquire Eric Cantona, the Frenchman whose exploits in his brief stay at Elland Road had fired the imagination. The 26-year-old Cantona cost Manchester United £1.2m, which must rank among the bargains of the decade.

Cantona was every manager's dream and every manager's nightmare; a regal talent subjected to the whim of a knavish temperament. Manna for the media, he made news whether scoring spectacular goals, aiming a kung-fu kick at an abusive spectator, or simply standing aloof with imperious disdain, nose and collar raised.

Signed in November 1992, Cantona was the catalyst as

218

United's twenty-six-year championship famine ended and Ferguson's progress through the nineties gathered momentum. The facts speak for themselves:

1990   First Division: 13th
        FA Cup: Winners.

1991   First Division: 6th
        European Cup Winners Cup: Winners
        European Super Cup: Winners
        League Cup: Runners-up

1992   First Division: Runners-up
        League Cup: Winners

1993   Premier League: Champions

1994   Premier League: Champions
        FA Cup: Winners
        League Cup: Runners-up

1995   Premier League: Runners-up
        FA Cup: Runners-up

1996   Premier League: Champions
        FA Cup: Winners

1997   Premier League: Champions
        European Cup: Semi-finalists

Peter Ball, who collaborated with Eamon Dunphy in writing the acclaimed *Only A Game*, the diary of a season, has taken a lifelong interest in Manchester United. Ball, of *The Times*, found that observing the team with Ferguson in charge evoked flavours of the Busby era:

'With four championships in five years, including the elusive League and FA Cup double twice, and the European Cup Winners Cup, League Cup and another FA Cup to boot, there is no doubt that Alex Ferguson stands comparison with his revered fellow Scot. No doubt also that his United stands comparison with the fifties United which, of all the sides, was the one that made United special.

'Ferguson's achievements have been immense, but perhaps the one which would give him most satisfaction would be the thought that the Babes would recognize this current side as their natural heirs. Roger Byrne would see Gary Neville as coming from the same mould; Eddie Colman would surely clutch Paul Scholes, that other bouncy Salford boy, as a brother; and if other parallels are less obvious, Duncan Edwards and David Pegg, Liam Whelan and Bobby Charlton would recognize Nicky Butt and Phil Neville, Ryan Giggs and David Beckham as kindred spirits, young men imbued with the spirit of Manchester United, and young men who relish the game and the battle. They may play for rich rewards, but they also clearly play for fun and glory.

'And that also reflects on Ferguson and his determination to restore the old ethos of the club which Busby developed. Perhaps his greatest achievement of all has been maintaining the primacy of football and of the right footballing values in a club which has become a multi-million-pound business empire in a sport which is now very lucrative, a far cry from the world Busby's young team lived in. A lesser manager, or a lesser man, might easily have let the business values take over. Ferguson has resisted. When he arrived in 1986, the club was not healthy, for all the glamour. He himself said that the changing room was more like a drinking club than a football club, and he recognized he had to make fundamental changes to the approach as well as to the team.

'It would be fair to say that initially, with the first team, he made his mistakes. New to English football, some of his early signings were less than convincing. Nineteenth when he arrived in November 1986, he steadied the ship so that the team finished eleventh. But a second place a year later was not the start of the recovery, and when the side slumped badly in 1989, the dissatisfaction in Manchester was almost tangible. At the time, Ferguson revealed the pressures he felt under in an interview with his close friend Hugh McIlvanney.

'His job certainly looked far from secure in January 1990

when United stood at sixteenth in the First Division and it was widely believed that defeat in the FA Cup third round at the City Ground would seal his fate. Instead, Mark Robins, one of the first of the young players to emerge from the restructured youth system, scored the only goal. United scrambled through to the final, via two wonderful, nerve-racking semi-finals with Oldham, and won it, beating Crystal Palace after a replay. A year later, the European Cup Winners Cup was added with the memorable victory over Barcelona. Ferguson had at last persuaded the directors to go for broke on a rebuilding programme, and the signings of Peter Schmeichel, Gary Pallister and Andrei Kanchelskis paved the way for the start of the glory days.

'But even while the early days yielded struggles and some grief on the surface, Ferguson was putting the structure into proper repair, particularly by rebuilding the youth programme. When he took over, Manchester City were sweeping up the best local talent, and the recruits from further afield were equally unexciting. He changed that, both by putting in a new team of scouts and coaches, and by his own involvement, talking to parents, and convincing them of his continuing presence in their sons' development. Suddenly, instead of joining City, Ryan Giggs was at United. Soon, others followed. The crop who won the FA Youth Cup in 1992 and reached the final in '93 must be the best since the team of Duncan Edwards and Eddie Colman; like that team, they have gone on to make United a great club once more. Like the Busby team, under Ferguson's influence they have been brought up with the right footballing values, and the right personal values too.'

Sir Matt Busby died on Wednesday 20 January, 1994. He was 84 and had had blood cancer for a number of years. His wife Jean died in 1988, six years after being diagnosed as having Alzheimer's disease.

Although restricted by health problems in his later years,

the old master witnessed the dawn of the team's renaissance under Ferguson. Busby travelled to Rotterdam for the Cup Winners Cup Final in 1991, and in 1993 he shared in the joy of the long-awaited championship triumph.

Many years earlier, Busby had said that his memorial is the three great teams he created in twenty-three years of managership. Were a reminder needed, Manchester City Council had renamed Warwick Road, which leads to Old Trafford, Sir Matt Busby Way. After receiving news of his death, thousands travelled to the ground in tribute and mourning, leaving flowers, red, white and black scarves, hats, rosettes, flags and other mementos.

On the following Saturday, a minute's silence was observed at all British football matches. Everton were the visitors to Old Trafford. The respect shown by their supporters earned them a Carling No. 1 Award from the Premier League's sponsors for 'their exemplary behaviour'. Ryan Giggs, of Wales, scored the only goal of the match to give United victory, but the day, like many others before, belonged to a Scotsman. A lone piper encapsulated the poignant mood.

The funeral took place on Thursday 27 January, a day of drizzle. Thirteen black cars and three buses formed the funeral procession, which was flanked by two police horses. The cortège stopped for two minutes beneath the stadium clock commemorating the Munich disaster.

In April that year a memorial service, open to the public, was held at Old Trafford. One seat, distinguished by a brass plaque engraved with the words 'Sir Matt', was draped in black ribbons.

'Nobody can ever write or speak about Manchester United without mentioning his name,' Eric Cantona wrote in his autobiography, *My Story*. 'You sense and feel that his blood runs through every vein of the club's body. I am pleased that I played in front of him, and that he lived to see United Champions once more.'

Bobby Charlton was knighted in June 1994 for his services

as an ambassador to football. He had been a United director since 1984, a role he combined with business interests which included a travel agency, a football-coaching school and work in the media.

Johnny Berry, whose talent and experience on the right wing was a feature of the pre-Munich team, died in Farnham, Surrey, on 16 September 1994. He was 68.

In common with many former players, Berry, whose career was ended by the Munich disaster four months before his thirty-second birthday, had found it increasingly difficult to identify with the sport he had been drawn to as a youngster. Aside from the pace of the game and some of the weird and wonderful tactics and terminology adopted by certain managers and coaches, the financial aspect had become mind-boggling.

The implications of the Bosman Ruling in September 1995 caused further tremors in the transfer market. Jean-Marc Bosman obtained a restraint of trade judgement from the European Court of Justice against the Belgian club Liège and UEFA. The ruling carried a recommendation that players would become free agents at the end of their contracts, and could then sell themselves, and that the restriction on foreign players would also disappear.

British football already had a strong cosmopolitan flavouring. The proliferation of foreign players – some were bought because they were cheaper as well as more skilful than their British counterparts – was developing into an industry. On the eve of the 1997–8 season, there were 126 overseas players with Premier League clubs, costing a total of £156.64m.

Salaries were commensurate with the rising costs. The £25,000 transfer fee United paid Birmingham City for Johnny Berry in 1951 would represent a weekly wage negotiated by some of today's leading Premiership players.

Going into the 1997–8 season, United's record transfer fee was the £6.25m paid to Newcastle for the striker Andy Cole in January 1995. The record fee received at Old Trafford was the £7m from Internazionale, which took the midfielder Paul Ince to Milan in June 1995.

In May 1997 the European Cup Final was held in Munich and survivors of the 1958 air disaster were invited by UEFA to attend the match between Borussia Dortmund and Juventus.

'They sat in a row on a stage and tried to describe how they felt,' Peter Berlin wrote in the *International Herald Tribune*. 'It was a strange and powerful mix of emotions. Sir Bobby Charlton, who went on to win the European Cup with United in 1968, spoke in a voice cracking with emotion. Albert Scanlon, one of the team's wingers, furtively flicked away a tear. Yet there was still the teasing and joking, the soccer player's defence mechanism, even on the darkest subjects.

'The most famous of the survivors finally spoke, his words at first catching in his throat. "There isn't a day that goes by I don't remember what happened and the people who are gone," said Charlton. "The fact that the players are not here and are never going to be judged is sad. They'll never grow old."'

Manchester United have undergone many changes since 6 February 1958, both structurally and in personnel, and more are bound to follow. But rest assured, the Busby Babes play on in the Old Trafford of a vivid imagination. Mark Jones leaps high in defence and heads the ball to Eddie Colman, who has snaked into space and is ready to start an attacking movement. Liam Whelan glides forward, and opponents are wary. Duncan Edwards starts to go, and opponents are frightened. Colman squares the ball to Roger Byrne, moving up on the left. David Pegg makes his run and takes a long, accurate pass from Byrne over his shoulder, controlling the ball as he strides before crossing it hard into the penalty area with radar perception. Tommy Taylor rises majestically to head another spectacular goal at the Stretford End.